Forty Years of Texas Storytelling

"This book is a *tour de force*—a wonderful snapshot of storytelling in Texas. I didn't want it to end. The history of the Texas Storytelling Festival is fascinating and beautifully written. And the stories that follow, from a broad range of tellers, styles, and experiences, are each gems in their own right.

"The stories range from educational to stirring, from humorous to mysterious. They are personal tales, folk tales, and historical stories, from a variety of different cultures, recognizing the fascinating quilt that is Texas.

"Many of the tellers have won a John Henry Faulk award. I smiled when I saw that, as I knew John Henry and his British-born wife Elizabeth when I first lived in Texas in my early twenties. I know that he would have loved these stories—many written for the ear and not the eyes, so you can almost hear them being told. He would have reveled in their charm, their variety, and poignancy. And so did I. I thoroughly recommend this marvelous book."

—**Geraldine Buckley,** storyteller and author

The iconic quilt displayed on the stage at each year's festival was created by Judy Berry of Jacksboro from colorful tee shirts representing the early years of the event.

Forty Years of Texas Storytelling

Historical and Contemporary Tales from Diverse Writers and Poets

Ted Parkhurst
Editor

Published by the Tejas Storytelling Association
In Collaboration with
Parkhurst Brothers Publishers
MARION, MICHIGAN

www.parkhurstbrothers.com

Consumers may order Parkhurst Brothers books from their favorite online or bricks-and-mortar booksellers, expecting prompt delivery. Parkhurst Brothers books are distributed to the trade through the Chicago Distribution Center. Trade and library orders may be placed through Ingram Book Company, Baker & Taylor, Follett Library Resources and other book industry wholesalers. To order from Chicago Distribution Center, phone 1-800-621-2736 or fax to 800-621-8476. Copies of this and other Parkhurst Brothers Publishers titles are available to organizations and corporations for purchase in quantity by contacting Special Sales Department at our home office location, listed on our web site. Manuscript submission guidelines for this publishing company are available at our web site.

Printed in the United States of America
First Edition, March, 2024
Printing history: 2026 2025 2024 8 7 6 5 4 3 2 1
Library Cataloging Data
Forty Years of Texas Storytelling
Edited by Ted Parkhurst
1. Tales
2. Tales–Texas
3. Texas Storytelling Festival
398.2
2024
2024 trade paperback and e-book

ISBN: Trade Paperback   978-1-62491-202-3
ISBN: e-book   978-1-62491-203-0

Parkhurst Brothers Publishers believes that the free and open exchange of ideas is essential for the maintenance of our freedoms. We support the First Amendment of the United States Constitution and encourage all citizens to study all sides of public policy questions, making up their own minds.

Interior and cover design by   Linda D. Parkhurst PhD
Acquired for Parkhurst Brothers Publishers and edited by   Ted Parkhurst

032024

Contents

Introduction

BARBARA MCBRIDE-SMITH

WELCOME TO THE WIDE WORLD OF TEXAS STORYTELLING. If you are a Texan, or if you know a Texan, or if you have ever been to Texas ... you can appreciate why Mac Davis sang, "Oh Lord, it's hard to be humble, when you're perfect in every way.[1]" Texans have an affliction of being proud and loud. Reserve and understatement are not Texas virtues. So, it's no surprise that our stories have a larger-than-life quality. In this collection, celebrating the fortieth anniversary of the Texas Storytelling Festival, you'll find more stories than you can shake a stick at. Whether they are about our kin, our folk heroes, our religions (football and gigantic crosses), or our fractured fairy tales, they will warm your heart, tickle your funny bone, and make you shake your head in wonder.

When I came to that very first Texas Storytelling Festival back in the eighties, I thought I knew what storytelling was. Turned out, I had only touched the tip of the

---

1 Mac Davis's song "It's Hard to be Humble, from the album, Stop and Smell the Roses

elephant's trunk. Sure, I had grown up with the hyperbolic stories told around my family's supper table. And, for almost twenty years, I had been a school librarian, so I had told lots of folktales, legends, and myths to my students. But the stories and the tellers I encountered at that first Texas Festival changed everything I thought I knew about telling stories.

Back in those days, Denton was a small, quaint, two-college town. I had zipped right past it on the interstate many times, going to and from my hometown, Waco. I never saw a reason to stop. Little did I know that Denton would eventually become a gathering place for storytellers from all over the state and beyond. That spring of 1986, half a dozen friends and I loaded up in a van and made the four-hour drive from central Oklahoma to Denton, Texas. We cruised around the gorgeous 1896 County Courthouse and admired the eateries and boutiques on the Square. I was particularly curious to know the history of McBride Music & Pawn on Oak Street.

Eventually, we arrived at the Denton Arts Center. The building was filled with other educators, actors, activists, writers, wanna-be storytellers, and a handful of storytellers who actually got paid for their work. We were greeted by Finley Stewart, the brilliant and daring young visionary who pulled out all the stops to get that festival off the ground. We heard The Folktellers (Connie Regan and Barbara Freeman), the "Scheherazades in Denim" I had read about in School Library Journal several years earlier. We listened to the magnetic Elizabeth Ellis, who

10

wasn't born in Texas but got here as fast as she could. My friends and I expected a fun and educational weekend, and we got way more than we bargained for. We were overdosed on charisma.

The biggest eye-opener for me happened at a workshop presented by Dr. Rosanna Herndon, Professor of Communication at Hardin-Simmons University. These were her words, as I remember them: "In every generation, there is one, and often ONLY one, repository for the family's stories. If you are that repository, you must tell those stories." For the first time, I understood that I was my generation's repository. I promised myself that I would sit down with my family elders, listen to all their stories, and do my best to remember them. That's a promise I kept, and it gave me new purpose and a whole new repertoire as a storyteller. I feel certain I was one of many who benefited a hundred-fold from that workshop.

Another fortuitous moment occurred at a lunchtime event called a "Story Swap." Everybody who wanted to tell a story to a sandwich-eating crowd at the Arts Center could throw their names in a hat. Two of my travel companions and I took a chance, along with a couple dozen other hopefuls. Five names were drawn; mine wasn't one of them. However, one of my colleagues was in the lineup. Just before her turn, she leaned toward me and said, "I'm not ready for this. You are. Take my spot!" Her kindness boosted my confidence, so I stepped to the mic, explained the situation to the emcee, and got permission to proceed. I told the

Greek myth, "Orpheus and Eurydice." It was a story I had told several times to my students back in Oklahoma. But that day, at the festival, I told it differently. Using what I had learned from Rosanna Herndon, I re-imagined it as a family story in which a wedding and a death took place in a snake-infested town in Texas. I was encouraged by the positive response from the audience. My students had usually liked my stories, but they had never applauded. Applause is addictive.

I went home from the first Texas Festival believing that my life was going to change. And it did. I was invited to be a featured teller at the second annual Texas Storytelling Festival in 1987. That invitation led to more festivals across the U.S. and to friendships that have lasted a lifetime. I was one of many Texas storytellers who were discovering their unique voices in the 1980s: Jeannine Pasini Beekman, Tom McDermott, Tim Tingle, Doc Moore, Gayle Ross, James Ford, MaryAnn Blue, Judy Nichols, Jay Stailey, and so many others. At that second festival, I got to know John Henry Faulk, the legendary folklorist and radio commentator who fought and won a courageous battle against McCarthy's blacklisting campaign in the 1950s. I was honored to be part of a community of outspoken, spew-out-your-beverage funny, and shirt-off-your-back generous people.

That community has multiplied and diversified itself to include every demographic of my humongous home state. At least a dozen regional festivals in the state, from the Panhandle to the Rio Grande, were inspired by the original mothership festival. Some lasted, some didn't, but they all did their best to keep making Texas proud. There are now guilds and conferences and virtual events in every nook and cranny of the state—all offspring of the original festival.

Molly Ivins wrote: "If Texas were a sane place, it wouldn't be nearly as much fun." As a born and bred Texan, I know this to be absolutely true. We are all a little peculiar. We add unnecessary syllables to words, we make up our own similes and metaphors, and we believe that a wretched excess of anything is just about perfect. For Texans, storytelling is a way of life. It's no wonder we gave birth to one of the first and best storytelling festivals in the country.

Long live the Texas Storytelling Festival!

Barbara McBride-Smith wears many hats—simultaneously! For more than forty years, she has worked as a teacher, a school library media specialist, a theological seminary instructor, a writer, and a traveling storyteller. In each of these professions, she has employed storytelling as an integral educational tool and a compelling art form. Barbara is a recipient of both the John Henry Faulk Award for outstanding contributions to storytelling and the Circle of Excellence Award for stage performance. She has been a headliner fourteen times at the National Storytelling Festival in Jonesborough, Tennessee, and has frequently served as a teller-in-residence at the Timpanogos Storytelling Institute and the International Storytelling Center.

A Word From The Editor

THIS BOOK HAS BEEN CREATED FOR YOU, THE READER. The TSA Fortieth Anniversary Book Committee, Jaye McLaughlin, Hank Roubicek, Peggy Helmick-Richardson, Chester Weems, and I, started with the idea to create a permanent record of the Tejas Storytelling Association's history and the forty years of the Texas Storytelling Festival. We quickly realized that we had zero chance of including all of those who made up our individual lists of "Texas Storytelling Greats." Remembering our initial objective, though, we realized that we could create a record—a book—that *represented* the breadth and scope of our movement at forty. That we have done.

A deep thanks goes to everyone who submitted a story, contributed a photograph, assembled data, bought a copy, donated a copy to their favorite library or school, or otherwise promoted storytelling in Texas over the four decades of our organization's life—so far. We expect that scores of TSA members and friends will purchase many copies of this book and resell them at their gigs and events. By doing so, we lift the organization that, in turn, lifts our art.

As editor, it has been my task to solicit stories, edit them, and arrange them into sections. In this, I've endeavored to be inclusive, encouraging, and a teammate. Over thirty storytellers have contributed stories to this body of work. In addition, there are over twenty tributes to pillars of the Tejas Storytelling community that have been contributed by members and friends. The stories in this volume represent the creative genius our audiences have experienced to at annual festivals over the last four decades.

A few of our contributors are not Texans (yet). That's because each year, the creative directors of the festival choose to add at least one teller from another state or country. Those "outsiders" add richness to our events, and their stories add texture to this anthology.

Managing this project has been a joy to me. I trust that reading the stories will be a joy to you.

Ted Parkhurst
Editor and lifetime TSA Member

My Story
and I'm Sticking To It:
A History

ELIZABETH ELLIS

THIS BOOK IS BEING PUBLISHED TO COMMEMORATE the fortieth anniversary of the Texas Storytelling Festival. If you have never been to a storytelling festival, you may be wondering what that is and what it's all about. The Webster's New Collegiate Dictionary says that a festival is "a time of celebration," "a feast," or a "program of cultural events or entertainment." In truth, the Texas Storytelling Festival is all those things. For those who are story lovers and story listeners, the Festival is definitely a time of celebration. Folks come from all over Texas and surrounding states to attend. Many of them look forward to it all year and plan their trip months in advance.

It is a feast as well. Not of food. Instead, it is a feast for the ears. A veritable banquet of action and eloquence. Much like a feast of food, a wide variety of treats are presented— but they are delights for the ears. Folk and fairy tales from

17

cultures around the globe fill the listener with wonder and delight. Stories of personal experiences or family happenings warm the heart and remind us of how much we have in common. Spine tingling stories of ghosts and spirits come out at night. Enormous lies are told to stretch the imagination and make you laugh uproariously. Tales of wisdom and spiritual understanding help us remember there is light in the darkness. In short, you will hear something for every mood, for every interest, for everyone.

In our media—and computer-saturated world—it may sound strange to you that people would come together to listen to stories. Just listen. If that does sound strange, remember that people have been listening to stories from time out of mind. Throughout human history, people have gathered together to tell stories and to listen to the stories of others. It is perhaps our oldest art form. And even in these computer-dominated times there is still a special magic to hearing someone spin a good story. It is one of the things that sets human beings apart from other animals.

Any arts event that continues for forty years makes a testimony to the passion that folks have for the art form it embodies. It must fill a need, or it would not have survived for such a long time in our changeable and fickle world.

So how did the Texas Storytelling Festival get started? What is its *origin story*? A young man named Finley Stewart worked at the public library in Carrollton, Texas. Zinita Fowler, the children's librarian, was a storyteller in her own right. She decided to bring The Folktellers, cousins Barbara Freeman and Connie Reagan Blake, from North

18

Carolina, to her library to tell stories. The Folktellers had a unique way of sharing stories in tandem. Finley fell in love with storytelling as soon as he heard The Folktellers. Their tandem style particularly impressed him. He formed a similar partnership with his friend, James Howard. They decided to call themselves The Storyweavers and began telling at schools and libraries in the North Texas area.

Finley, the visionary, began planning to bring The Folktellers back to North Texas to headline a major storytelling event. A group of folks who surrounded Finley did the considerable work of putting on the first Festival. Finley was the trailblazer, the big-picture person. Finley's friends Sylvia Pitchford and James Howard were the willing workers. Dr. Ted Colson and Dr. Rosanna Herndon were the calm, steadying influences that kept things from flying off the rails. Although Finley deserves a great deal of credit for originating the Festival, in truth, the work of each member of the team was important.

To the delight of eighty-four listeners, the first Texas Storytelling Festival was held in Denton at the Denton Arts Center in 1986. The tellers were Dr. Rosanna Herndon, Dr. Ted Colson, Zinita Fowler, The Storyweavers (Finley Steward and James Howard), The Folktellers (Barbara Freeman and Connie Regan Blake), and myself. Except for The Folktellers, every teller lived in Texas. There are probably people who think that there was no storytelling happening in Texas before that first Festival, but that is not the case. There was storytelling happening all over the area, but the storytellers did not know one another. One of the most important accomplishments of the first Festival was how it drew the tellers together and made us part of one another's lives. The Festival became the net that caught us and drew us all together.

I was astounded to receive an award at that first festival "for a significant contribution to storytelling in the Southwest." Later, that award would be named the John Henry Faulk Award in honor of a well-known and much-beloved Texas storyteller who was a champion of freedom of speech.

At the second Texas Storytelling Festival, Barbara McBride Smith, then a librarian from Oklahoma, told a story that included some strong language. Although the language was appropriate for the story being told, one of the audience members took offense and an unpleasant confrontation occurred. This experience resulted in a great deal of discussion about freedom of speech, and artistic integrity. The organizers decided that no censorship of storytellers' presentations would ever be tolerated.

From the beginning, a commitment was made to bring in tellers from a wide array of ethnic backgrounds which might lead to greater cultural understanding. African American griot Baba Ayubu Kamau, luminous Navajo storyteller Sunny Dooley, keeper of Jewish wisdom stories Penninah Schram, and noted Japanese teller Hiroko Fujita are examples of a few of the people Tejans would have little access to without the presence of the Texas Storytelling Festival. Their influence was not just limited to those who heard them tell at the Festival. Their presence influenced the community of Denton as well. Once in the early days of the Festival I was given the opportunity to host national treasure, Mary Carter Smith. I picked her up at the airport and drove her to Denton to check her into her hotel room. She was dressed in beautiful Afro-centric clothing at a time when that was a rare thing to see in North Texas. After helping her get her luggage to her room, I walked back through the lobby on my way to my car. The eighteen-year-old young man who had checked her into her room stopped me. "Who was that?" he asked. I said that was Mary Carter Smith, one of the best-known and most respected African-American storytellers in the country. He replied, "I didn't know who she was, but I knew she was a *lady*." In my mind, I saw an image of ripples fanning out over the area.

By the conclusion of the second Texas Storytelling Festival, two things had become abundantly clear: the event had outgrown the Denton Arts Center, and there was a need for an organization to sponsor the event. After a great deal of discussion, because nothing done by storytellers is ever accomplished without a great deal of discussion, the name Tejas Storytelling Association was chosen. The historic spelling of the name was chosen because it derived from a Native American word that meant "friend." In the old maps of the area, the territory that is now Oklahoma was included. The name was chosen to show that although the organization was based in Texas, everyone in the area who was interested in storytelling was a friend and was welcome.

The Festival moved to tents that were set up on the

grounds of Texas Woman's University. One of the most memorable experiences happened while the event was being held on the grounds of the university. It was a cold March day, with a blowing wind that had a bite to it. In the middle of the afternoon, while Tom McDermott was on stage, the sprinklers came on under the chairs of the folks on the left side of the audience. The folks on the right side thought that was hysterically funny until the sprinklers came on under their chairs as well. Folks scattered like a coven of quail! My daughter, R.E.O., had the presence of mind to dash forward and cover the water flow with over-turned trash cans weighed down with folding chairs. This prevented damage to the sound equipment and musical instruments. However, most of the audience was soaking wet. We told everyone we were shutting down until the evening concert.

Since it was Spring Break, it took a long time to find anyone who could shut off the sprinkler system, which was, of course, set on a timer. While guys with pickup trucks went in search of farmers who had hay to sell, organizers found rags and dried off all the chairs and equipment. A thick layer of hay was laid down to absorb the water and keep folks from walking in the mud. The chairs were put back in place, and we were ready to begin the evening concert on time. That story could be used as a metaphor for the entire history of the storytelling festival because whenever there are bumps in the road, we handle them and do not allow them to hinder our mission of sharing stories.

Finley was patterning the Texas Storytelling Festival

after the National Storytelling Festival in Jonesborough, Tennessee. An array of nationally recognized tellers graced the stages of our Festival: Jackie Torrence, Donald Davis, J.J. Reneaux, David Holt, Kathryn Tucker Windham, Syd Lieberman, and Jay O'Callahan, to name only a few. Unlike the National Festival, Finley also believed that the storytellers in our own area were the equal of any in the United States, and so tellers from our region were presented mixed in with those of national reputation. Several now-prominent tellers got their first shot at a festival audience on the Tejas stage, among them Tim Tingle, Barbara McBride Smith, Lynn Moroney, Donna Ingham, Sheila Phillips, Tom McDermott, Toni Simmons, MaryAnn Blue and Eldrena Douma. [Editor's Note: Elizabeth Ellis self-effacingly declines to note here that, as an already-acknowledged national teller at the time, her involvement was and continues to be a guiding presence for the Festival and the Tejas Storytelling Association.]

Workshops were added because Finley believed that our region was so large that enticing folks to come to one event a year was such an accomplishment that we ought to try to teach them something before they headed back home. He also thought that it might be easier for teachers and librarians to get permission to come to the event if there were workshops which would make it possible for them to do a better job of sharing stories when they returned home. This proved to be true, and we are proud to say that we still offer continuing education credits for attending the workshops that we offer.

For years, the Festival has kicked off on Thursday evening with a concert of Ghost Stories. Perhaps "ghost stories" is too small a name. "Scary stories" would be a more accurate descriptor. Over the years we have shivered to ghost stories, both historical and imaginary. We have been horrified by tales of witches, vampires, and zombies. Monsters from the folklore of many cultures have come to menace our dreams. Literary tales from the strange imaginings of writers such as Edgar Allen Poe and H. P. Lovecraft have haunted us. It has been, and remains, one of the most popular concerts of the Festival. The stories begin with those that are "family-friendly" and get progressively scarier as the evening advances. This allows parents to decide when it is appropriate to take their children home. Due to the generosity of Joe "Doc" Moore, it has been one of the parts of the Festival that is free and open to the public. That tradition has remained in place out of respect for Doc's memory.

One of the most beloved parts of the Festival is the Sacred Tales concert held on Sunday morning. When you attend this event, you may hear stories from the sacred texts of many different religious traditions: Christian parables, Sufi tales from the Muslim tradition, Zen riddle stories to ponder, the tales of the Bal Shem Tov, or other wisdom stories from the Jewish tradition. Perhaps there will be stories of Native American spirituality or the wisdom of African dilemma stories. Or perhaps someone will share a tale of their own search for religious truth. Or maybe you will hear a family story of dedication and sacrifice. Each year the stories shared will be quite different. Yet each of them will inspire you and challenge you to live a more useful life. A part of the concert will be "The Passing of the Basket." Unlike other services which pass the basket to ask you to contribute, the basket will be passed so that you may take something to help you remember the experience and what you learned from it. Flowers, musical instruments, and plastic insects are examples of things taken from the basket over the years. Many of these small objects find places of honor in the homes of the listeners in attendance.

Although it has been tweaked a few times over the years, the mission statement of the organization remains the same in its focus. *The Tejas Storytelling Association is a non-profit organization dedicated to fostering an appreciation of storytelling as an oral tradition, a performing art, and an educational tool.* All the activities of the Association are scrutinized to determine if they further the mission statement of the organization. It was decided that our flagship event, The Texas Storytelling Festival, effectively fulfilled the first two parts of our mission statement, but more should be done to help accomplish the third part: storytelling as an educational tool. The Texas Summer Storytelling Conference was developed to help those who used storytelling in their work to build their skill set. The programming of the Conference was centered around the needs of teachers, librarians, clergy, attorneys, counselors of all types, as well as professional and amateur tellers. The Conference has proven to be an excellent experience for professionals and paraprofessionals to continue their storytelling education. It has developed a reputation for providing outstanding workshops, seminars, and panels. Many who attend say exchanging ideas with those who do the same kind of work they do is invaluable. It is held every other year in even-numbered years and rotates around the state to give more people easy access to it.

Native Texan John Henry Faulk was a nationally-known storyteller and radio personality with his own hit radio show *Johnny's Front Porch* on CBS when he ran afoul of Senator Joseph McCarthy during the Cold War. McCarthy and his minions at the for-profit corporation AWARE, Inc. were searching under every bed and in every closet for people they felt were Communist sympathizers. As a member of the board of directors of the American Federation of Television and Radio Artists (AFTRA), John Henry tried to stand up for those whose lives and careers were being destroyed by McCarthy's blacklisting. That put John Henry squarely in the sights of their notorious machine. Overnight, John Henry went from being one of the best-paid artists on the radio to being unemployable because he had been labeled a Communist. Unlike others who struck deals to their own benefit or sold out their friends and coworkers, John Henry sued the blacklisters. It took seven years for the case to go all the way to the Supreme Court, but when it did, he won the largest libel suit in American history to that time.

This experience, which would have made a weaker man bitter, inspired John Henry to become a student of the First Amendment and a champion of freedom of speech. He was the undisputed hero of many storytellers in our organization, especially Finley Stewart. The board of directors of the Tejas Storytelling Association voted to name their most prestigious storytelling award in his honor.

This award is presented each year at the annual Festival, and the recipient has traditionally been kept a secret until the presentation occurs. In 1990 the board decided to present the award to Finley himself. That was long overdue. Wishing to remain secretive about the presentation required a great deal of skullduggery. Since Finley was the Executive Director, it seemed like an impossible feat. But a plan was devised to pretend to present the award to someone else. It even involved having a plaque prepared with Zinita Fowler's name on it to keep Finley from being suspicious. Finley had arranged for John Henry Faulk himself to be a featured teller at that year's event. It was a glorious moment when John Henry presented the award named in his honor to Finley. It was made even sweeter by the fact that Finley was gobsmacked by the experience.

The entire storytelling community was deeply grieved when John Henry Faulk died of cancer the following month, April of 1990.

At the tenth anniversary festival, seventeen tellers from Texas and the surrounding states were asked to return to share their stories. The Folktellers were asked to make a return visit to celebrate this auspicious event. It would have been difficult for many of us to imagine that, in the future, we would be able to invite twenty-five tellers to return to our stage to celebrate the Twenty-fifth

Anniversary and even thirty-five favorites from past years to commemorate the Thirty-Fifth. Looking back at what has been accomplished is a source of pride. Looking forward to the Fortieth and beyond is a source of anticipation and joy.

What could be more traditionally Texan than a Liars Contest? Remember all those old guys who used to sit outside the general store or on the benches in front of the county courthouse and entertain one another with the most outlandish yarns they could dream up? The Liars Contest at the Festival is a direct descendant of that folk heritage. Many lies are intended to fool people. This is *lying for entertainment.*

The Liars' Contest was added to the lineup of the Festival in 1997. It has proved to be one of the most popular storytelling concerts. Folks come from all over the state and surrounding territory to throw their hats in the ring. The winners get bragging rights. Some years they receive ugly trophies from sports in which they did not participate. Of course, the trophies would be lies! You wouldn't expect truthful items to be distributed at a fibbers event, now, would you? Some years there are actual cash prizes, depending on the budget for that year.

Liars' Contests have traditionally been a competitive form of storytelling that appeals mostly to men, a part of the boasts and brags that flourished on the American frontier. For years storytellers James Ford and Jay Stailey swapped the title back and forth between themselves. However, eventually, the ladies decided they wanted to be in on the fun. It was rich when now-legendary liars Donna Ingham and Sheila Phillips began giving the guys a run for their money. The judges have included some of Denton's outstanding citizens: the mayor, council members, attorneys, clergy. The tales are evaluated on originality and believability as well as presentation.

Finley served as the Executive Director of the Tejas Storytelling Association and the Director of the Texas Storytelling Festival until 1997, when he stepped down to become a full-time professional storyteller. Chairperson of the board of directors and longtime Tejas supporter, Karen Morgan, became the Executive Director and Festival Director. Karen was a strong leader of considerable charm and savvy who understood the importance of developing strong relationships between the residents of Denton and the City of Denton and our mission. She invented ways to involve the local Denton residents and get them involved in storytelling. The "Raising the Bar" event gave local lawyers a chance to show off their storytelling skills and brought a number of new supporters into the Association. During Karen's tenure, a ghost story event held on the courthouse lawn attracted a large number of local families and especially delighted the children.

Karen Morgan also reached out to local maven Martha Len Nelson to organize the Denton Storytelling Task Force. Nelson worked tirelessly to advance the causes of the Association to the City and its leadership. As the head of the Task Force, Martha executed an annual fundraising dinner and auction to benefit the organization. The members of the Task Force, such as Peggy Capps, Carrell Ann Simmons, and Dalton Gregory, also represented the organization to City leaders and civic groups, helping us receive critical financial support. The importance of the work of these dedicated, well-connected, and influential citizens cannot be overstated. Their support created an era of refreshing financial stability in our history. Deep pocket support from the City of Denton established financial stability for the organization and the Festival. Because of her exceptional service to the Association, the Special Service Award was renamed the Martha Len Nelson Special Service Award in her memory.

During Karen Morgan's leadership, Solina Marquis began to produce and organize field trips to the Festival for students from the schools in North Texas. Teachers and librarians were eager for their students to have this fantastic enrichment opportunity. A tent was added to the festival plan at Quakertown Park to be able to seat all the school, library, and community groups that wished to attend. Friday's daytime programming was focused on the students, with regional tellers supplementing the work of the featured tellers.

All the years that the Festival was held under tents, we had to be mindful of the weather. There is a saying, "If you don't like the weather here in Texas, just wait a minute. It will change." That is true all year long, but it is particularly true in March. We never knew if there would be heavy rains or brilliant sun. Folks might be running to the merchandise tent one year to buy umbrellas; the next, it might be sweatshirts to bundle up against a March thunderstorm. But with the help of the Site Director, Gene Helmick-Richardson, we always seemed to overcome whatever was thrown at us.

Then there was the Year of the Tornados. Thursday night Ghost Stories were blustery, but that seemed to fit the feel of the evening. Friday morning, however, turned out to be another matter. There were fifteen hundred students on the grounds when the first sirens went off. Fortunately, Dan Keding from Illinois was no stranger to tornados. He understood what the sound meant at once and gave instructions to the children to follow him to cover in the nearby Women's Club Building. Some of the teachers took their children directly to the buses and back to school as soon as they received clearance from their principals to do so. The majority of the students and teachers followed Dan to the Women's Club Building to wait out the weather. By the time my legs could make sure all the students had cleared the tents and gotten to the Women's Club Building, the students were packed together like sardines, and Dan was already singing with them to keep them focused and entertained.

Later that afternoon, the Denton Fire Department would make us evacuate the tents when the sirens sounded again. It was the supper hour, but no one was allowed to leave the Women's Club Building to go in search of food. Tim Couch and I had been preparing a light supper for fifteen or so people who were to attend a meeting to be held in the Women's Club Building. We were going to give them soup and cookies. I had purchased a big bottle of V-8 Juice for my own use during the weekend. Since you could get a second one for just a few pennies extra, being the thrifty type, I had bought a second one as well. When the entire listening audience came to the building, I began to pour the V-8 Juice into the vegetable soup. Tim raided the refreshments intended for a party for the festival volunteers later in the weekend. The end result was that everyone got something to eat. That event has been referred to as "The Feeding of the Five Thousand" or the time of "Loaves and Fishes." But Scripture aside, there were no loaves or fishes—just soup and cookies. Folks were so happy to get something to eat they did not realize they were eating V-8 Juice with spoons.

Later that evening, we received permission to return to the Main Stage Tent. However, the rain began again shortly after the first teller took the stage. With no tornado warnings, we were not required to evacuate, but the rain kept pelting the overhead canvas harder and harder. Before long, the rain on the roof of the tent was so loud it was impossible to hear the storytellers. One of the featured tellers booked for that year was the deaf teller Peter Cook. Peter often tells utilizing a voice interpreter since his speech is limited. However, I knew he could also tell stories using sign language without speech but with plenty of communication. I quickly changed the order of the storytellers and sent Peter up on the stage. He told eloquently, using nothing but his body. It was breathtaking. And the noise the rain made was immaterial.

Then our dear Betty Berkey, former President of the Association, slipped in the mud. She hit a tent stake and broke her pelvis.

The idea of making the Festival an indoor event made immediate sense to everyone. We moved into the Civic Center the following year and have been hosting the Festival there ever since. If any of the TSA board ever wax poetic about being in the tents, someone else will immediately recount the harrowing story of evacuating the tents for safety's sake. The nostalgia soon passes.

Supplementing the Civic Center with the nearby Public Library and the Women's Club Building has allowed the festival to host all the elements of our "full-service Festival," except for the student field trips. Since it had become difficult to bring students to the Festival, we decided to transport a part of the Festival to the students. Our "Tellers in the Schools Project" was born to make sure that students in Denton schools would continue to hear stories. The program made it possible for hundreds of Denton children to hear stories each year. Betsy Mosier was the first manager of the project, followed by Genie Hammel, who still leads it today.

Saturday morning continues to bring our Kids Day Activities for children and their parents or grandparents. A concert by tellers with deep experience in telling to the young is followed by workshops, story swaps, and pizza for the young folks. There are a number of our members who specialize in working directly with children who want to learn to tell stories themselves. Sue Kuentz, MaryAnn

Blue, Toni Simmons, Traphene Hickman, and Vivian Rutherford have given countless hours to this aspect of our Association's work. Each year when we hear the children share the stories they have prepared, we know there is no reason to worry about the future of storytelling in Texas.

One of the successes of Karen Morgan's time as Executive Director was the inclusion of sign language interpreters in our events. Kate Lauder and Joel Hill collaborated to make storytelling concerts accessible to the hearing-impaired. Later Libby Tipton from Tennessee would join them. The addition of these talented signers deepened the story experience for the hearing audience as well, giving lots of opportunities to be moved to laughter by the comic faces of the interpreters or to tears by the poignancy their elegant movements added to the stories.

Word of Karen Morgan's skills reached the national storytelling organization, and they invited her to join their board of directors. Karen resigned as Tejas's Executive Director to serve on the national board. We sought a new Executive Director and found Cristin Thomas.

Times got tough for non-profit organizations, and Tejas found itself in debt. Many people thought we would need to claim bankruptcy at that time. In fact, many people in Denton believed we would fold up our tent and steal quietly away into the night. I was once again President of the organization. I drove to the homes of each member of the Board of Directors to speak to each of them face to face. I learned that each one felt we should try to continue the work of the Association. To dispel rumors that we were going under, I authorized the planning of a Texas Summer Storytelling Conference. After all, you don't have a big event if you are going under, now do you?

I sent a letter to all the people who, historically, had been vested in the organization: past board members, leaders of the affiliated storytelling guilds, and significant volunteers. I invited them to the Storytelling Conference to attend a Council of Elders, which would determine the future of the organization and the Festival.

At that meeting, those who attended were asked to go to a large blank wall and post their concerns on butcher paper. Board members organized the ideas and issues that were posted into ten different categories. Then the members were asked to go and stand beside the idea or concern they felt was most important to them. Of course, one of the ten was "Should we declare bankruptcy?" When people were asked to break into groups by standing beside the idea or concern they most wanted to work on, no one stood next to "Should we declare bankruptcy?" Every single person present chose one of the other issues or projects listed on the wall. Each group sat down together and began to organize and brainstorm around the issue or project that they had chosen.

At the end of the day, I was asked when we were going to vote on whether or not we were going to claim bankruptcy. Some of the members of the group were astounded when I pointed out to them that they had, in fact, already voted. No one had formed a group under "Should we claim bankruptcy?" Everyone had chosen to work on something that had to do with the future of the organization. They had voted with their feet and with their ideas without realizing it.

The mettle of the members was made clear then. People followed through on the commitments that they had made at that meeting. It wasn't easy, but we paid off the debt. We doubled down on making donations to the organization. We programmed our way out of debt, taking on a new festival in Abilene. Local groups put on fundraisers for the state organization. We increased the number of grants for which we applied. Just two years later, at the annual membership meeting held each year at the Festival, I used a laptop to make the last payment of the debt in front of the entire membership. They all deserved to be present for that moment because they had all participated in our success. It was one of our proudest accomplishments.

One of the results of the belt-tightening because of the debt was the realization we could no longer afford to pay an Executive Director. Christin Thomas left, and the Tejas Storytelling Association became an all-volunteer organization. Don't get me wrong, we have always had amazing volunteers. Names like Marvin Brown and Harry Berkey stand out in my mind immediately. Now much more volunteerism was necessary. The work formerly done by the Executive Director now had to be accomplished by the Board of Directors. They moved from making policy to overseeing and implementing every element of the organization's mission. Countless service hours have been given to ensure the success of the festival and the organization's other programs.

Each year the festival is put on by a multitude of volunteers. Some go to the airport to pick up tellers arriving from out of state. Some move tables and chairs during the event. Some carry the trash to the dumpsters or supervise the recycling. Others like photographers Paul Porter and Chester Weems have given us a lasting visual record of our events. It would be hard for a person who has never put on an event like this to imagine the many tasks that need to be organized and accomplished for the event to run smoothly. Without those who have tirelessly worked to publicize the event, there would be no event to attend. You can't go to an event if you don't know that it is happening. Peggy Helmick-Richardson and Kim Lehman have devoted long hours to organizing our marketing campaigns.

Although every volunteer's work is essential and appreciated, they would not know what was to be done without the planning of the Festival Team. Every person who has taken a leadership role or served on the Festival Team has donated a piece of their life to the event. Those who have served as Artistic Director or Managing Director of the Festival will get to stand in the express lane when they go to heaven. I am sure of it!

No matter how diligent your planning, there will always be problems you could never have foreseen. For years, the festival was held the last weekend in March. I was the Festival Director and was sure that every detail had been tended to when, in 1997, the NASCAR folks built the largest racetrack in America eleven miles away and took our traditional weekend. Thousands of people would be invading the relatively small town of Denton. I knew there would not be hotel rooms for our listeners or a place to get a table at a restaurant in the entire area. You wouldn't even be able to drive to Denton without encountering road-block-level traffic. With a weary but determined heart, I asked the Festival Team to begin planning from scratch so the festival could be held on a different weekend. The only dates the Civic Center had available were for the second weekend in March. Since that year, the event has been held annually during that weekend.

That experience pales in comparison to what occurred in 2020. The television news reports were filled with stories of the COVID-19 infections spreading across the country. Of course, we had no idea how bad it would become. Folks began arriving for the festival, and the Thursday night Ghost Stories went off without a hitch. On Friday, I was grabbing a bite of lunch with the Artistic Directors Toni Simmons and MaryAnn Blue when I received word from the City of Denton that the mayor was closing all City-owned buildings because of the spreading infection. We would need to vacate the Civic Center completely by six o'clock that afternoon—Mayor's orders.

A flurry of activity began. Toni and MaryAnn began immediately calling those people who were still in transit to the festival, telling them to head back home. As Managing Director, I went to speak with the manager of the Civic Center. I am not embarrassed to admit that I begged that we be given more time. There were tears involved, as I remember. I was able to negotiate to be able to continue our festival programming through the evening concert. I breathed a huge sigh of relief when they agreed to allow us to dismantle and pack out on Saturday morning.

Toni and MaryAnn went to work reorganizing the programming. They tried to put as much of the festival event into the time remaining to us as possible. The rest of the day was a non-stop storytelling marathon. They were amazingly successful at giving so many tellers a chance to share the stories they planned to tell. Then the sad work of pack-out began early Saturday morning. Like everyone else, we thought the lockdown would end in a few weeks. Of course, that would not prove to be the case.

Even the Covid lockdown could not stop the Texas Storytelling Festival. The board quickly approved moving to a virtual format. The first Festival presented through Zoom showed us the need for a new type of volunteer: media-savvy folks who could do the technological work necessary for a smooth and professional event. Now attendees did not have to live in Texas or the adjoining states. Folks from as far away as Alaska could attend. Some were even from foreign countries. We began to build listener relationships that could not have been imagined before.

Naturally, we were sure that there would only be one online Festival. However, it soon became clear that the lingering virus would make a second online festival necessary. Everything we had learned during the first online-only festival was put to effective use in the production of the second one. The technological gurus—Brooks Myers and Dean Keith—made the transition to online programming both possible and effective. Although the lockdown caused by the pandemic is over, virtual programming continues because it allows us to reach out to larger audiences.

The Texas Storytelling Festival is continually growing and changing, a living part of the oral tradition in the United States and beyond. Throughout the years, we have been open to change as the storytelling community has grown and evolved. More tellers began to share personal experience stories. As time went by, the subject matter of some of the stories people wished to share became more challenging. Not everyone had a happy childhood. "Valley of the Shadow of Death" experiences needed to be shared. The Main Stage needed to remain "family friendly." The Fringe concerts were instituted to give voice to important stories that may not be for every listener.

Edgy material is welcome. Dark subject matter is appropriate. Bravery is applauded. The Fringe concerts at our event conform to the rules for fringe events throughout the country: tellers are chosen by lottery ahead of time. You never know what you are going to hear. It is the luck of the draw. Some tales of family dysfunction may be followed by stories of racism, betrayal, or struggles with cancer treatment. What you can know ahead of time is that every story will be heartfelt and shared openly and honestly.

Throughout the nationwide storytelling community, there was an increased focus on telling short, true personal stories. This vein of stories tended to draw a younger crowd who appreciated competition. The Story Slam was added to the festival lineup to showcase this genre of telling. There is an announced theme for the stories to be shared. Judges choose winners based on a point system for presentation, relevance to the theme, and story crafting. The Slam has proven to be a popular addition to the event and has drawn some fresh faces into our group.

As I write this, the 2023 face-to-face festival is coming up. We are eager to be together, but plans continue for the production of online programming.

The Texas Storytelling Festival is like a family. Like most families, we are eager to spend time together. Like most families, we have elders and new arrivals. There are kissing cousins and black sheep. Sibling rivalry and occasional family spats flow and ebb.

Like any other family, if you asked two different members about the family's history, you would likely get two different versions of the same occurrence. That happens in families all the time. So, this is my version of the history of the festival and the organization that produces it. If you asked any other Tejas family member, they would probably remember different things, and have seen happenings from a different perspective. But I was asked to write a history for this book, so it is my account of what happened.

That's my story, and I'm sticking to it!

Story Themes

These symbols are used above story titles
to help identify stories by theme.

PERSONAL & FAMILY

TRAVEL

HISTORY

CULTURES

HUMOR

TALL TALES & SCARY STORIES

FOLKLORE

HEROS & SHEROS

Guns, Hats, and a Bucket of Chicken

BERNADETTE NASON

THERE'S A BUMPER STICKER THAT READS, "I wasn't born in Texas, but I got here as fast as I could," and I always say with a laugh, "that it doesn't refer to me." I never planned to come to Texas. If you'd told me I was going to end up in Texas, I would've laughed and laughed and laughed. But I had always wanted to come to America, the land of opportunity, the land of new beginnings.

And boy howdy, was I ever looking for a new beginning. Actually, I was looking for a new me—a new, improved me, and this was not the first time. I had tried to find a new, improved me in Africa. However, after eighteen months in Libya, I was still shy and lacked confidence, but I learned how to smoke cigarettes and make wine in a bucket. Clever girl!

I had searched for a new, improved me in the Persian Gulf, but after five years in Dubai, all I'd learned was how to work a ten-hour day, a six-day week, and I still had low self-esteem and high anxiety. If I'd changed anything, it wasn't for the better. Frankly, I was more lost than ever. Thus, in 1992, I made the grand life decision that, just two weeks after leaving Dubai for the last time, I would become the new me in the New World. United States of America, here I come!

The reason I came to the Lone Star State was to spend *one week* with the only person I knew in America. You see, I was on my way to Los Angeles to become a movie actress. Yes, I'd decided that the best way to combat shyness, lack of confidence, low self-esteem, and high anxiety was to go to Hollywood and spend time with the beautiful people. Clever girl!

My friend, Mary Ellen, had gone to the University of Texas in Austin, and—like many before her—she had loved Austin so much, she never left. Our mothers had been pen-friends since the 1940s. When Mary Ellen and I were old enough, we became pen-pals too. In the early 1980s, Mary Ellen backpacked through Europe and stayed with my family in England. She always said I was welcome to do the same thing in the US. Well, I truly hoped she meant it because the choice was made. I was on my way.

As I sat in the plane on that first flight from England to the States, I realized how blasé I had become. It was as if nothing surprised me any longer. After my time in North

44

Africa and the Middle East, I felt I was culture-shock-proof. I sat there with my airline gin and tonic in hand and thought about what I'd done to get me to this point: I had sold my house, sold my car, sold my boyfriend—no, I just left him—no one would've given good money for him. I had gathered my money, bought my ticket, and here I was. Some folks thought me brave, selling my worldly goods and heading for yet another unfamiliar land; others thought me stupid. I teetered on a tightrope between bravery and stupidity, and I was finding it harder and harder to distinguish which was which. Like an act at the Cirque de Soleil, on one side there was a bottomless pool of blue sparkly water; on the other, mud and crocodiles. I tried not to think at all.

I was due in Houston in the early evening with a short break before the local flight to Austin. After a scary landing—one of those white-knuckled, eye-popping, stroke-inducing landings—it was clear there were weather issues. Now, for all my travels, I'm not a good flier. I still believe that group willpower gets the plane off the ground, and fervent prayer lands it. When there's turbulence and fear grips me, I've been known to hold the hands of fellow passengers so hard, they've winced with pain. I once threw my arms around the man sitting next to me and snuggled with him for an hour, so great was my need for comfort. It was embarrassing at that point having to introduce myself.

Houston was engulfed in fog, fog so bad that all flights were grounded, and passengers were sent to hotels for the night. The metaphor of being lost in the fog was not lost on me! And I do hope that the *irony* of an Englishwoman arriving in America on a foggy night isn't lost on you. You know, don't you, that Americans are always teasing Brits about English weather? Everywhere I travel in Texas, I get a hard time, especially about the fog. London smog, people say. "Like pea-soup," they say. To quote one of my favorite Texans, Dr. Donna Christopher Ingham, "So thick you can cut it with a knife ..." To quote another great Texas storyteller, J. Frank Dobie:

> It is as dark as the inside of a cow here in the city of Cambridge. In London it is as dark as a burglar's pocket. In many another place in England it is as dark as the back corner of a bear's den. If glass were not so fragile, I'd take a jar outside and let a sample of the fog settle into it and send it home. The fog hereabouts comes up from the Fens, they say—the Fens that the Romans were building a road across two thousand years ago. The trains are creeping through the fog hours late. Last night the buses all stopped running. I thought about the drivers of the army trucks and cars forever on the move, shifting between east and west, north and south, as ceaselessly, it seems, as currents of air everlastingly unstabilized between frigid and torrid. The dark is thicker tonight than it was last night. Maybe it is too thick to carry the sound of motors in the sky. At least, I have not noticed the throb on a plane for hours.

I'm telling you, nothing compares with Houston fog. It's an entity: a great, smothering blanket of grayness, like something from a Stephen King novel. Nothing was visible as we landed; nothing at all. My first memory of Texas is of walking from the shuttle bus to the hotel and being soaked from head to foot before I even stepped through the door. I thought I might be dripping with sweat; I knew in October, temperatures could be in the 90s. But I didn't expect to be dripping with *fog*. In England, we're discombobulated by fog, disenchanted with fog, depressed even by fog, but we're never *drenched in fog*. Everyone said things were big in Texas, but I wasn't expecting Big Fog.

Next day, the sky was blue, and the sun was shining, but due to circumstances connected with my luggage, and the unexpected loss of it, I didn't set out for Austin till late afternoon. But here I was at last, and there was Mary Ellen to meet me. Ah, Mueller International Airport! I always loved the fact that it called itself international. Perhaps it didn't quite understand what the term "international" means. But that was Austin—weird from the very start!

As we waited for my luggage, I looked around me. Where were the guns that I'd heard so much about? Everywhere I'd ever lived, people talked about America and its guns: the availability of guns, the murder rate, the number of prisons required to accommodate misguided gun users. These were subjects that the rest of the world discussed regularly. I had lived in some scary places, but I'd never lived where ordinary citizens were allowed to carry firearms. I didn't expect to see everyday folks carrying automatic weapons (oh, how times have changed), but I definitely thought I'd see handguns in holsters. I couldn't see any.

I wasn't disappointed; I was more surprised. Where were the guns, then? Were they in people's pockets? Handbags? Up their trouser legs? I found myself eyeing everyone suspiciously, staring at body parts. I looked at Mary Ellen. Did she have a gun? I didn't want to ask her—it might embarrass her. It might upset her. She might shoot me!

As we dragged my luggage cart away from the carousels, I saw a police officer standing at the exit, generally keeping an eye on proceedings. He had a gun in a holster! My first totally-visible-to-the-human-eye, ready-to-shoot-me American gun! I thought about English police officers—who are not allowed to carry guns, in case you didn't know—with their truncheons (you know, those little black sticks they carry on their belts to defend themselves against the angry mob). I realized how charmingly pathetic they must seem to Americans. I found myself staring at the policeman's gun. I couldn't take my eyes off it. Suddenly the officer put his hand on the holster.

"Everything alright, ma'am?" he said. I giggled like a silly schoolgirl. And I was through that door like greased lightning, lickety-split, like a bat out of the proverbial, emerging into the blinding sunlight of an October evening in Austin, the state capital of Texas.

Now I can't tell you exactly what I expected because I didn't realize until the gun incident that I had any preconceived ideas at all. Culture-shock-proof, remember? But I must say that when I walked out of the airport, I thought there would be more hats. And by hats, I don't mean baseball caps, backward or otherwise. I don't mean straw hats, sombreros, ladies' sunhats, or fabulous flowery church hats. I mean, I'd been to the movies; I'd seen some fabulous Texas hats. No, no, no. By hats, I mean, Stetsons, ten-gallon hats, *cowboy* hats. There wasn't one, not one single cowboy hat to be seen. Had I landed in the wrong state? Wasn't this Texas? Wasn't this cowboy country?

I did see a kind of cowboy a week later at an Austin nightclub called *Dallas*, now demolished and, alas, being replaced by an apartment building. These were strange cowboys—tall, thin, and almost uniformly dapper, like cartoon cowboys. They wore tight, well-ironed blue jeans with razor-sharp creases down the front ending at concertinaed denim on ornate cowboy boots. Their crisp shirts were so starched they couldn't move their torsos except to lift their arms to dance. They danced an odd, rather un-masculine dance called the two-step. They kept their hats on indoors, which struck me as a bit uncouth. My mother wouldn't have approved.

But I digress. Frankly, I was rather disappointed that there was no fiesta to greet me, no hoedown in my honor. And as we drove away from the airport, I was still searching for a John Wayne look-a-like when Mary Ellen asked me what I'd like for supper.

"What are my options?" I asked.

"Well, we've got some great restaurants, or we could get a bucket of chicken to go."

"A bucket of chicken?" I was picturing a large, metal pail with a dead rooster hanging out of it. She told me about KFC and Churches' and their large containers of fried chicken.

"Any veggies?" I ventured.

"Yep," she said, "There's corn on the cob, French fries, or mashed potatoes and gravy."

She pulled into a 7-Eleven to get gas. I waited in the car while she filled up. A young man came out of the store carrying a large plastic bucket in his hands. Oooohhhh, a bucket of chicken!

I leaned out of the car window. "Mary Ellen, look, that guy has a bucket of chicken."

"Nope," she said, "that's not chicken. That's a Big Gulp."

At first, I couldn't work out how much drink there would be in a sixty-four-ounce bucket. Then I remembered my mother's Pyrex measuring jug ... Sixteen ounces equals one pint. Which means sixty-four ounces is—four pints! Two quarts! That poor kid was going to drink half a gallon of name-brand cola! That sounded like some sort of torture. Don't you have to drink sixty-four ounces of Gatorade when you have a colonoscopy? If I drank sixty-four ounces of highly caffeinated soda, I could swim the Atlantic faster than Wonder Woman; I'd win Olympic Gold in the 10,000 meters; I could knit a sweater in eight minutes, and I can't even knit.

We ended up in Threadgills—sadly, also now gone, a victim of the pandemic. Threadgills was, as many will know, a Southern-style restaurant and something of an Austin tradition. It acquired the first beer license in the county in 1933. Janice Joplin cut her teeth there in the 1960s. Bernadette Nason had her first American meal there on her way to Los Angeles in 1992!

Now, Americans often call English things "quaint." But to me, Threadgills was quaint ... and a bit ... well ... shabby. A coat of paint wouldn't have gone amiss. The cutlery was cheap looking. The crockery was mismatched. I didn't know then that Austin was famous for its shabbiness. That shabby was Austin's middle name. Austin knew that shabby was chic before "shabby chic" was fashionable.

You've got to cut me some slack here. Please remember I'd been traveling for days. I was hot, tired, and irritable. I was disgruntled before "disgruntled" was fashionable. I wanted fish and chips, apple crumble with sweet yellow custard, and a nice cup of tea. I wanted my Mummy!

I looked at the menu through tear-filled eyes. There was something called *Catfish and French Fries* which looked a lot like Fish and Chips. There was something called *Apple cobbler a la mode* which looked a bit like Apple crumble and custard. I was just looking around for the Texas equivalent of a nice English cuppa when a waitress arrived.

"Iced tea, hon?" she said, placing before me a large glass, dripping with condensation, along with a basket of fresh, sweet-smelling breads wrapped in a red checkered napkin. I took my first bite of succulent Southern cornbread (would Kathryn Tucker Windham have approved?) and my first sip of sweet Texas tea. All of a sudden, everything took on a new light. Things looked different, and I started to feel a little bit better.

I sniffed back the tears. *All right,* I thought, *perhaps there are one or two little things that can surprise me*

51

culturally. In my attempt at self-improvement, I managed a year and a half in Africa and five years in the Middle East. Surely I can begin this new journey with a week in Austin, Texas. This is as good a new place to start as any." As I took another sip of tea and reached for a second piece of cornbread, I could feel myself smiling. I could feel a new leaf turning. And, as I write this thirty years later, I realize that I was, after all, a clever girl!

Bernadette Nason is an award-winning actor, writer, voice-over artist, workshop facilitator, and storyteller (Texas Commission on the Arts touring roster since 2002). A celebrated author, Bernadette has written two memoirs, *Tea in Tripoli and Stealing Baby Jesus.* She has performed multiple solo shows but probably best known for appearing in *Miss Congeniality in 2000.* She's worked in England, Libya, and Dubai, and lives in Austin (30 years and counting) with her beloved ex-husband and some questionable cats. Photo by Sam Bond.

Nancy Hanks

KATHY HOOD CULMER

DO YOU KNOW NANCY HANKS? Have you ever heard of her? Well, neither had I before I was well into my adult years. That's when I learned that Nancy Hanks was Abraham Lincoln's mother (Lincoln was the sixteenth president of the United States).

As a child, though, I had met a Nancy Hanks. For real! I must have been seven or eight years old when I did, and boy, was I excited!

I had wanted to go down there and meet her for a long time. I'd heard her sound so many times as she'd bellowed her call each and every day for as long as I could remember, announcing her arrival and departure. Why, if you were anywhere nearby as she sped in and out of town, there's no way you could miss her call. Then, finally, the day came!

There I was with my Aunt Bea, with my heart racing in anticipation of the ride I was about to take.

Now, before you get too carried away trying to figure out how old I must be to have met Abe Lincoln's mother, let me clarify. The Nancy Hanks I met was not the mother of this nation's sixteenth president. My Nancy Hanks was a train. And what a beauty she was! Instead of dressing in those dark steam engine colors, she had adorned herself in shiny blues and other colors that announced her arrival almost as loudly as the whistle of her engine. From the vantage of a seven or eight-year-old small-town girl, she was the longest train in the world, but compared to the passenger trains of today, the four to six cars she ran would seem relatively minuscule for a train.

It was my first train ride. No longer would I have to wonder what it would be like to ride in one of those big steel blue cars, whose wheels turned and churned because I was about to experience it for myself—from the inside. "The wheels on the train go round and round..." I couldn't wait!

"All aboard!" the conductor called.

"Ready, Baby. You're not scared, are you, "my Aunt Bea asked.

"No, ma'am, I'm not scared." My heart was racing, and I was grinning. I can guess that part without even remembering, because every time I would get excited about something, my heart would go racing, and I would start grinning. They still do.

We took our seats on the train. Aunt Bea let me sit by the window so I could look out and see some of that big wide world that existed beyond the limits of the small town where we lived.

The conductor took our tickets. Although folks' recollection of the cost varies, all agree that round trip, the tickets never cost more than two dollars and change. In those days, you could take your seat before they took your ticket because I guess folks weren't so worried about being "taken." Chug chug, chug chug. Choo Choo. The wheels on the train go round ... We were on our way to Atlanta, Georgia.

I didn't know back then why that train was called "the Nancy Hanks," but I found out many years later that the Central Georgia Railroad actually named her Nancy Hanks II after a racehorse by that name. I could only guess that because she was named the II, at least some thought must have been given to the first Nancy Hanks. It was not until I was living in Indiana and was asked to tell stories at Lincoln State Park in Spencer County in a room called the Nancy Hanks room that I began to make any connection between the train of my youth and the mother of a president. As a little girl, seated in my seat in the "Colored" car of that train, I had yet to learn of the president who signed his name to a decree that would call for some of my enslaved forebearers to be set free.

I didn't know or care anything about the Jim Crow laws we were living under at the time that put limitations on the choice of seats on the train that day. We could ride in the front car of the train, but only because the front car came after the engine. In all other vehicles of public transportation, however, we had to ride in the back. But none of that concerned me that day because I was going to ride the train to Atlanta with my Aunt Bea.

Seated there on the train, between my Aunt Bea and the window on my right, we departed the Broad Street Depot at 12:30 p.m. That was the daily departure time for the Nancy Hanks. From the time of the Second World War, I was told, until the mid-1960s, the Nancy Hanks train made daily runs from Atlanta to Savannah, with stops in Griffin and Macon along the way. The route was always the same. The time was always the same. And the train cars, which held about fifty passengers each, would almost always be full.

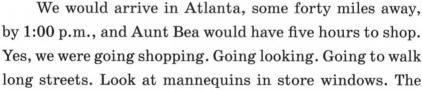

We would arrive in Atlanta, some forty miles away, by 1:00 p.m., and Aunt Bea would have five hours to shop. Yes, we were going shopping. Going looking. Going to walk long streets. Look at mannequins in store windows. The Mannequins seemed to say, "Come on in and see. Come on in and buy." Five hours to shop before the conductor's call.

Aunt Bea and some of her shopping friends were such regulars on the train that if they happened to be running close to 6 o'clock, the "colored" conductor (that's how African Americans were referenced at the time) would wait for them at the top of the steps that led down to the tracks where Nancy Hanks waited to carry them home. Then, when he spotted them coming, he would make his final boarding call.

No need that day, though, because we were there in plenty good time. Aunt Bea had also gone to the beauty shop, and I'd gotten to watch her and the other ladies as they were all prettied up. I liked that part, too. That was almost as much fun as the shopping that would come later because I enjoyed watching other people. I liked looking at and listening to grown people talk. I liked seeing and being in the presence of people you didn't see every day and all the time.

But shopping was the main thing we had come to do that day, and it was, for sure, *the best* part of the trip. With shopping, you still got to see people, but you also got to look at, try on, and fancy yourself in all sorts of pretty things. You got to touch them, feel them, and see yourself all dressed up in them. It was *so much fun*, even if you didn't get to take it home with you.

I don't remember what Aunt Bea bought me that day, but I know she bought me something. Riding the train was just part of the reason my heart had beat in such anticipation of this day. Going to Atlanta, which I thought was the biggest and best city in the whole wide world, was just part of the reason. Knowing that I was going to get to see lots of people doing all kinds of things was just part of the fun. But knowing that my Aunt Bea was planning to buy me something to take home with me undoubtedly contributed to some of those extra heartbeats.

And, now, with whatever she had bought me, all tucked and folded and stuffed inside her bags, with five hours of shopping—minus the time it had taken her to get her hair done—behind us, with feet and bodies tired, with far less racing of the heart, and with a grin resigned to a smile. "The wheels on the train go round and round." Nancy Hanks pulled out of Terminal Station in Atlanta, Georgia, at 6 o'clock on the dot, and we were on our way home.

Had I been a more frequent rider of that train, had I been older or more informed, Had I known to care about such things, perhaps, I would have been excited or impressed by the fact that Dr. Martin Luther King, Jr. and Martin Sr., aka, Daddy King, Dr. Ralph David Abernathy, and others who had worked tirelessly and sacrificially in the Civil Rights Movement also rode the Nancy Hanks train. Probably, they had ridden it that year, maybe even that month. They would definitely ride it again. From Atlanta to Savannah.

My Aunt Bea said she recalled riding it with them on some occasions. They and so many others rode it as a means of transportation, of course, but they also rode it as a form of protest. They rode it so that we and others who looked like us might not be limited in choosing where to sit on the train next time.

When I was talking to Aunt Bea, trying to recall events for this story, I asked her if Dr. King and others in the movement ever sat in the passenger cars designated for "Whites Only," and she answered, "One time when it was getting pretty hot, they did." I later wondered about that *getting hot* part, whether she meant the temperature or the movement.

Dr. King and other foot soldiers in the war on injustice in the segregated South rode the Nancy Hanks train so that African Americans might not only be able to ride the train, but so that we could also have access to all sections of the train and enjoy the same amenities available to white passengers, such as the dining car that was reserved for "white passengers only."

When I asked a former white politician from my hometown why the train stopped running, he answered, without hesitation, "Lack of passengers." Then, he added, "They say they quit having good service in the buffet car and the dining car. They had always had good food service."

We, as African Americans, had not known of the good food service. The porter came through the car to which we were assigned seating carrying food in some contraption across his shoulder that held snack treats like crackers, peanuts, and that kind of stuff. Peanut butter crackers and a drink were fine for me that day as I rode to Atlanta on the train to go shopping with my Aunt Bea. As a child, when my appetite was greater for the wonder of the world and the joy of my first train ride, it didn't take much to make me happy.

When I learned that Nancy Hanks was Abraham Lincoln's mother's name, I thought, "Wow, isn't it ironic that this southern train that had made daily runs from Atlanta to Savannah, there in the heart of the old confederacy, was named after the mother of the "Emancipation President." When I was told the train was named after a racehorse, I was disappointed. It was not the story for which I was hoping.

But, you know what? The irony is still there. Because you see, the train that I rode as a girl, and the train that so many others rode for twenty-five years or more, there in the heart of Georgia, was called by the same name as the mother of the president whose policy and politics had ignited a major war between the North and the South and had contributed to the eventual demise of the South's beloved institution of slavery. And there was, at the very least, the subtle suggestion that it was the efforts of those who sought to bring about an end to segregation on this train that contributed to *its* demise.

The wheels on the train no longer go round.

Kathy Hood Culmer is an author, storyteller, speaker, and teacher committed to delivering words of encouragement, truth, and inspiration. Kathy has told stories and presented workshops in many venues, including churches, schools, festivals, and retreats. She has performed at the National Storytelling Festival, Duke University's Mary Lou Williams Center for Black Culture, the Texas Storytelling Festival, and has been the featured teller at the Network of Biblical Storytellers' International Festival Gathering, as well as the Canadian Biblical Storytelling Gathering. She is the editor of *Yes, Jesus Loves Me: 31 Love Stories*, and is the author of *On the Wings of Prayer*, a collection of prayers and inspirations, as well as "Big Wheel Cookies: Two for a Penny," published in *The Rolling Stone and Other Read-Aloud Stories*.

Bending the Arc Toward Justice

Dalton Gregory

THE TEXAS STORYTELLING FESTIVAL has been held in Quaker-town Park for more than twenty-five years. This story is based on actual historical events in Denton, Texas.

A vote to erase the Quakertown community happened in 1921. Forty-five years later, in 1966, there was a similar vote to dismantle the Solomon Hill neighborhood. The two votes had very different results. The story includes histor-ical and fictional characters. The main character is Rose Lee Jefferson from a book titled *White Lilacs*, written by Carolyn Meyer and published in 1993. Ms. Meyer has graciously shared Rose Lee to connect Quakertown to Solomon Hill. I am grateful to Carolyn Meyer and recom-mend her book to you.

"Oh Lord, it is hot. Let's get out of this unaircon-ditioned house and sit on the front porch. At least there is a little breeze out there." Jim William (named after his great-grandfather) knew that his mother, Rose Lee Jefferson, was right.

"Mama, I'll get a damp rag to clean the dust off the furniture."

"Much obliged, Jim William. Porch furniture always has dust, but especially so living on a dirt road in a whole neighborhood of dirt roads. It seems like dust is always a problem here on Solomon Hill. Well, except when it rains—and then the problem is mud."

It was after supper, and the day's heat still lingered on Hill Street. A few neighbors joined Jim and his mother, Rose Lee, on that front porch enjoying the shade, the slight breeze, and glasses of sweet iced tea. They were visiting and catching up on other neighbors. And wondering if that new bunch of folks elected to the Denton City Council was going to deliver on their promise to pave the streets in their neighborhood.

"I'm trying not to get my hopes up that something good will come our way from City Hall," said Rose Lee. "It seems like lots of promises get made by folks running for office, but after they get elected, they either forget or replace the promises with excuses. If they had to battle the extremes of dust and mud in *their* neighborhood—well then, it might be a lot harder for them to forget."

Jim said, "But do you think they will forget how many of us on Solomon Hill voted them in and the old establishment council members out? It seems like they have been paying more attention to us since we helped defeat that 1966 bond election last year. Had it passed, it would have destroyed our neighborhood."

Mrs. Kimble had just joined the gathering on the porch. She brought a platter filled with slices of fresh pound cake to share. When Jim mentioned the 1966 bond election, Mrs. Kimble got all wound up, just like when she and other ladies who were part of the Women's Interracial Alliance were going from door to door all around Solomon Hill, registering folks to vote in that election.

Mrs. Kimble said, "I'm glad the voters didn't forget what a double-dealing scheme they were trying to pull in that bond election. Can you even imagine trying to use tax dollars to buy up our entire neighborhood, sending all of us packing to who knows where, bulldozing all our homes, and then selling the land to developers? They said it was 'urban renewal,' but it was really *neighborhood destruction.*"

Mrs. Kimble continued, "They called Solomon Hill 'blighted.' It was City Hall that blighted it by refusing to pave the streets or provide streetlights. They even refused to run trash collections through the neighborhood. Every house had to have a burn barrel to deal with trash. Can you even imagine labeling Solomon Hill as blighted? Thank goodness lots of white voters with principles joined us in defeating that shady deal."

Jim added, "Well, I heard that some white folks voted against the bond because they were afraid Black folks might end up living in their neighborhoods. But they voted no, and I'm glad that deal is dead."

Rose Lee looked at the group, gave a little sigh, and then looked at Mrs. Kimble. "Did you just ask if I could imagine a bond election passing that would destroy our neighborhood? Did you really ask if I could imagine everyone in our whole neighborhood having to move?"

"Now, Rose, you know that 'can you imagine' is mostly a figure of speech? We all know *you* can imagine. You don't even have to imagine it since you lived it back in 1921."

Now you know how it goes with folks visiting on porches. One story leads to another. Stories get repeated even when everyone has heard them before. But some stories need repeating, so we don't forget.

Rose Lee never needed much to prompt her to tell her family and neighbors about what happened in April of 1921 when the voters of Denton passed a bond election much like the one that failed in 1966.

Rose Lee began, "Quakertown was what we called our neighborhood. The name was chosen to honor the Pennsylvania Quakers who had fought to abolish slavery in the 1850s and '60s. I loved growing up there. I lived with my parents and my brother. Down the street was where my mama's people lived. My grandmother cleaned houses for white folks, and my grandfather Jim William was a talented gardener. He had a special talent for growing white lilacs. I loved sketching pictures of the flowers he grew in his yard and in the yard of the wealthy white family who lived over on West Oak St. We called that street Silk Stocking Row

64

because of all the big fancy homes."

Rose Lee continued her story, "Quakertown was where two different branches of Pecan Creek joined together. By 1920 more than fifty families were living there. Quakertown had stores, restaurants, a doctor's office, a mortuary, and three churches. The churches took turns each year hosting everyone in Quakertown to dinner on the grounds to celebrate Juneteenth. Quakertown was called a 'Freedman's Town' because it was started by enslaved people freed after the Civil War.

"Our home was an easy walk to the town square where the stately courthouse sat surrounded by a nice green lawn shaded by pecan trees.

"But it was still hard for Black folks in the 1920s, especially in the South. Jim Crow laws put many restrictions on Blacks. The KKK had lots of influence. The Daughters of the Confederacy had just erected a statue on the courthouse lawn to honor Confederate soldiers for the effort to support what they called 'the noble cause.'"

It said so right on the plaque.

My mother heard the white ladies she worked for call it the "War of Northern Aggression" because they thought "Civil War" sounded coarse. The folks in Quakertown understood: that statue was actually put there to remind us that white folks were still in charge.

With that, Rose Lee just shook her head, sighed deeply, and then told more of the story to the folks sitting on her front porch.

"I was just an eleven-year-old girl then in 1921. But

I heard all the grownups talking about the upcoming bond election. The town's white leaders wanted approval to buy up every house in Quakertown, every business, and the churches too. They wanted to clear out every black person from the neighborhood. They said it was to build a park, but there were plenty of other places to build a park without having to destroy any neighborhoods.

"While serving a meal at the house where she worked on Silk Stocking Row, my mother heard the president of the girl's college telling a luncheon guest that Quakertown needed to go. He said it was undesirable to have black folks living so close to the college. He even said it was unsafe. He was saying all that with my mother right there in the dining room, refilling his glass of iced tea. He made it plain that, to his way of thinking, my mother, all of our family, and all of our neighbors were undesirable!"

Jim interrupted, saying, "Did you all hear about Seneca Village in New York City? Back in 1857, it was declared 'blighted.' The city bought up that entire neighborhood of Blacks to build Central Park. First, they planned on buying up property owned by rich white folks, but they were powerful enough to stop it."

"But momma, why didn't the Quakertown people organize like Blacks are doing now? Why didn't they vote against the bond issue?"

Rose Lee replied, "Remember, I said the KKK was active in Denton? And the Jim Crow laws made it almost impossible for Blacks even to register, much less actually to vote. My older brother did speak up, and they tormented him something awful."

Rose Lee continued, "The 1921 bond election passed. For every vote against, there were two votes for it. Soon after, officials started going to each house in Quakertown and telling the owners what they would be paid for the land. No negotiations. They would also get a small amount of money if they wanted to move their houses to a new neighborhood. But that neighborhood, Solomon Hill, was southeast of town—literally on the other side of the railroad tracks.

"About half the folks in Quakertown moved to Solomon Hill, but it was never the same as Quakertown. Many families left altogether. Most went north hoping that the grass was greener up there."

Here Mrs. Kimbell broke in, "I hope none of them moved to the Greenwood Neighborhood in Tulsa. It was only five months after the Quakertown vote that the Tulsa massacre happened."

Rose Lee's son Jim said, "Those were awful hard times for Black folks."

"Yes indeed," said Rose. "Families were torn apart when they cleared out Quakertown. Many of the Black businesses didn't reopen. Our Black doctor left town and the state. My best friend moved. My grandmother Lila wasn't leaving her house. She didn't either. The night they jacked it off the foundation and started moving it to Solomon Hill, she sat right on her front porch the whole night. I sat on that porch with her at my grandfather's request."

Rose Lee Jefferson said, "Most folks that enjoy that

park along Pecan Creek today don't realize how many people got hurt when they destroyed our Quakertown neighborhood. When they tried the same shenanigans to move us out of Solomon Hill, they didn't even try to sweeten the deal with another park."

Jim William suggested, "I guess they were so arrogant that they didn't think they needed any more incentive. They must have thought moving the Blacks would be reason enough."

Mrs. Kimble said, "Well, for sure, they didn't count on our work to register voters to fight the bond. Thank goodness President Johnson made good on President Kennedy's goal and the dream of Dr. King by getting the Congress to pass the 1965 voting rights act. That made it a lot easier to get registered voters in Solomon Hill. And for them to actually go vote."

Rose Lee added, "And we voted the next year to get rid of the council members who promoted that scheme. The new folks promised to get services to Solomon Hill. But I'm beginning to doubt that they will make good on getting our streets paved. I'm tired of the dust or the mud."

Mrs. Kimble said, "Oh, you haven't heard, have you? Our Women's Interracial Alliance is helping to make it happen. They are going to start paving the streets in a few weeks. The city council did their part, but some of the white absentee landlords didn't want to pay their share to get the streets paved. They collect rent whether the streets are paved or dirt."

One of the white ladies in our group, Trudy Foster,

did some research at the county clerk's office to see which folks were holding things up. All our Black neighbors who own their homes agreed to pay their third of the cost for paving the street in front of their houses. The city would pay a third of the cost, and the folks across the street would pay the other third.

It turns out the holdup was because of several absentee landlords in Mrs. Foster's own church. She used one of the bulletin boards in the church fellowship hall and posted the names of those church members under pictures of their rent houses. Called them out and embarrassed them. It only took a few days for them to pay their share of the paving cost. Oh—and get their names off that bulletin board."

Rose Lee said, "Bet they didn't have to go borrow any money like the rest of us did to pay our third. I guess Rev. King was right when he said, 'The arc of the moral universe is long, but it bends toward justice.' I just wish it didn't take quite so long."

Jim William added, "You know, Mamma, that arc doesn't bend by itself. It takes good people working hard to bend it. It takes laws to guarantee our right to vote and then us actually getting out and voting."

It took the Women's Interracial Alliance to organize, register voters, do the research, and convince folks to do the right thing.

In 2007, the City of Denton decided to recognize the past by renaming the park along Pecan Creek "Quakertown Park." A sculpture honoring the Quakertown community was installed in the Denton Civic Center located in the park.

In 2021 an installation honoring The Women's Interracial Alliance was placed in another park. That group was first organized in Denton in the early 1960s. It consisted of Black women and white women—mostly church women. They had started meeting together to understand each other better and to fight segregation and discrimination toward Blacks. They alternated meeting in the homes of white members and black members. They became friends and got to know each other's families. They set up afterschool tutoring programs, registered voters, worked for progressive candidates, and then held them to their campaign promises. And through their efforts, the arc of the moral universe bent a bit more toward justice for all.

Dalton Gregory is a native of Denton, Texas, and a retired educator who has worked in the Austin, Houston, and Denton school districts and at The University of North Texas. Experienced, adaptable, and unique, Dalton has told stories in schools, churches, around campfires in the San Juan Mountains of Colorado, and in his neighborhood barbershop. Committed to TSA, he is currently on the board and, since its inception, has missed only one Texas Storytelling Festival. Photo by Walter Eagleton.

Tseg'Sgin' Gets A Job

GAYLE ROSS

IN THE EARLY 1960s, Jack and Anna Kilpatrick traveled throughout the Cherokee hills in Northeastern Oklahoma, collecting and recording stories from a wide variety of storytellers. Both were Cherokee themselves and spoke fluent Cherokee, as did the storytellers. The Kilpatricks published many books on Cherokee medicine and lore, and the stories they collected were published in *Friends of Thunder—Folktales of the Oklahoma Cherokee*. Among these tales are stories of a character called Tseg'Sgin', who does not appear in earlier collections recorded by James Mooney and others from the Cherokees in the Eastern homeland. When writing Cherokee in phonetic English, "e" is sounded as the long "a" and "i" as the long "e," so Tseg'Sgin' would be pronounced Jayg'Sgeen'.

The Tseg'Sgin' stories possess features that are either European, post-contact, or both. The Kilpatricks speculated that Tseg'Sgin' may have the African-American character, High John the Conqueror, as a prototype, while conservative Cherokees they interviewed pointed to the similarity of the name Tseg'Sin' to Andrew Jackson, the ultimate symbol of trickery and deceit. I think that the Appalachian Jack tales are a significant influence on the Tseg'Sgin' stories.

Folklorists and storytelling aficionados will recognize Foolish Jack and the decidedly unCherokean motif of the King and the Melancholy Princess. In the Jack tale, Jack lives with his mother, while here Tseg'Sgin' lives with his grandmother, his *Ulisi* (you lee see.) I love the Tseg'Sgin' stories because they demonstrate the way Cherokee stories grow and change like the Cherokee people themselves do.

One morning, Ulisi woke Tseg'Sgin' very early. *"Choog,"* she said. "You may be just a boy, but you are old enough to help me with the things we need. Go out today and find a job, and don't forget to bring the pay you receive home to me." So Tseg'Sgin' got up, dressed, and went out to see what he could find. He loved to watch the boats on the river, and he often had good luck fishing there, so that's where he went first. Now, it happened that there was a man who owned both a warehouse and a flatboat used to ferry travelers across the river. There was so much traffic for the ferry that he found it difficult to keep up with the work of running the warehouse. When Tseg'Sgin' asked if he had any jobs available, the owner was glad to hire him to ferry people across on his flatboat. "When the people get off the boat, they will pay you with whatever they have," said the owner. "If they have coin, you give that to me, but anything else they give you is yours to keep."

Tseg'Sgin' worked hard all day, loading people and goods on the flatboat, ferrying them across, and unloading them on the other side. Most people that day had money which Tseg'Sgin' gave to the owner. At the end of the day, one woman paid him with a strong needle with a goodly length of thread attached. Tseg'Sgin' carefully put the needle on top of a nearby log while he helped the woman unload her goods. But when he went back to get the needle, the wind had covered the log with a pile of fallen leaves. No matter how much he sifted through the leaves, he could not locate the lost needle. When he went home that evening and told Ulisi what had happened, she said, "Foolish boy! You should have pinned the needle to your jacket and brought it home that way."

"*Howa,* ok," said the boy. Next time, I'll do that."

The next day went very much like the first. At the end of the day, a group of travelers paid Tseg'Sgin' with a fine fat pig. Tseg'Sgin' undid the clasp on his silver gorget, picked up the pig, and tried to stick the pin through the pig's skin! The pig squealed and began to kick and struggle, knocking Tseg'Sgin' to the ground and ripping his clothes to shreds! By the time Tseg'Sgin' could get to his feet, the pig had disappeared into the woods. When he got home and told Ulisi what happened, she said, "You are so foolish! You should have tied a rope around his neck and brought him home that way!" "Howa," said Tseg'Sgin' "Next time, I'll do that!"

The next day, traffic on the river was very slow. Tseg'Sgin' only ferried two men and their horses, and both of them paid money to the owner. Finally, as the sun was going down, a family with their wagon arrived, and Tseg'Sgin' helped them load, ferried them across, and helped them unload on the other side. The man was a farmer who paid Tseg'Sgin' with a large, colorful rooster. Thinking back to what Ulisi had said, Tseg'Sgin' took a piece of rope and tried to put it around the rooster's neck! But the rope was thick and unwieldy, and as he struggled to get it around the rooster's neck, the rooster flew up into Tseg'Sgin's face and scratched him with his sharp spurs!

Tseg'Sgin' dropped the rope, used his shirtsleeve to wipe the blood from his eyes, and saw the rooster disappearing into the woods. When he got home, while Ulisi was rubbing salve on his scratches, he told her all that had happened. "I have a fool for a grandson," sighed Ulisi. "You should have used a thinner cord and tied the rooster's legs together. That way, he couldn't have scratched you, and you could carry him home slung over your shoulder!"

Howa," said Tseg'Sgin' "I'll do that next time!"

The next day, two families moving west arrived at the ferry. They each had a wagon piled high with their possessions, as well as several horses. It was hard work helping to load the wagons, all the household goods, and the horses on the flatboat. After Tseg'Sgin' ferried them across the river and helped with the unloading, he was given a fine black horse for his pay. Remembering what Ulisi had said, Tseg'Sgin' took a thin piece of cord and tied the horse's legs together. He struggled all afternoon to sling the horse over his shoulder, but the horse was far too heavy! The horse finally grew impatient with Tseg'Sgin' and began buckling and kicking! The thin cord around his legs snapped, and the horse ran off into the woods! Once again, Tseg'Sgin' arrived home empty-handed and had to explain to Ulisi what he had done.

"You are such a fool," scolded Ulisi. "You cannot carry such a large animal, but the horse could have carried you! You should have ridden him home!"

"Howa," said Tseg'Sgin'. "Next time, that's what I'll do!"

The next morning, when Tseg'Sgin' arrived at the ferry, a man with a herd of cattle was already waiting to cross. He paid Tseg'Sgin' with a fine fat cow. Tseg'Sgin' thought back to what Ulisi had said and decided he would ride the cow home! "I hold on to a horse's mane when I ride a horse," thought Tseg'Sgin'. "But a cow does not have a mane. She has a tail, though, so I should ride backward and hold on to her tail!" It wasn't easy to jump up on the cow, but Tseg'Sgin' finally managed it, and he took a firm hold on the cow's tail! The cow bucked a little, let out a bellow, and began to gallop away as fast as she could! Tseg'Sgin' held on to the tail for dear life and let her run. Because he was facing backward, he couldn't see where they were going! The cow ran straight down the main road into a large, prosperous city!

There was a wealthy king living in that city. This king had a daughter who had never laughed in all the years she had been alive! She had never so much as smiled! The king became worried about his daughter and brought all the city's young men together. "If you can make my daughter laugh," said the King, "you can marry her, and I'll give you half of my kingdom." So, when Tseg'Sgin' on his cow rode into the town square, there were hundreds of young men, all playing the fool, doing silly things and behaving as goofy as they could in hopes of making the Princess laugh. When she saw Tseg'Sgin' riding backward on a cow, she laughed so hard that tears came into her eyes!

Seeing her laugh, all the young men began to clamor that she was laughing at them! "She was laughing at me," each of them said. Soon, they were all arguing over who the Princess was looking at when she began to laugh, and then they began to fight! All the young men were fighting in the street!

The King stepped down into the square and called for quiet. "Let the Princess tell us who made her laugh," said the King.

"It was the man riding backward on the cow," said the Princess. "I never saw anything so funny before."

The cow hadn't even slowed down as she ran through the town square, so the King sent some of his men to follow the cow's tracks to see what had become of the man who had made the Princess laugh. They found the cow, who had grown weary after her long run, and they found Tseg'Sgin' still astride and clinging to the cow's tail! "Do you know what you have done?" said one of the King's men.

"I don't know what I did," said Tseg'Sgin'. "But whatever it was, it was the fault of this silly cow. I couldn't make her go where I wanted!"

"You have just won a rich Princess for your wife!" said another of the King's men. So, the King's men told him all about the Princess who never laughed and how she finally did when she saw Tseg'Sgin' on his cow.

"The King has said you can marry her," said one of the King's men. "And he will give you half of his kingdom. You are very lucky, and soon you will be very rich too!"

Well, Tseg'Sgin' thought back to every piece of advice Ulisi had ever given him, but he couldn't remember anything she had ever said about having a rich wife. *Still*, thought Tseg'Sgin', *a rich wife seems like a good trade for this stubborn cow. When you ride her, she only goes where she wants!* So, Tseg'Sgin' returned to the city to meet the King and his soon-to-be bride. Luckily, Tseg'Sgin' and the Princess got along tolerably well, and he sent a King's man to bring Ulisi to the city.

Tseg'Sgin' and the Princess were married in a lavish ceremony. The feasting and celebrations went on for many days. The first thing Tseg'Sgin' did after the wedding was to build a fine new house where he, his bride, and Ulisi could live together.

So, despite his foolish ways, Tseg'Sgin' became a wealthy man, and he didn't need to work at the ferry anymore. Ulisi thought that was a very good thing since she still believed her grandson was not really cut out to hold a job!

Gayle Ross is an enrolled citizen of the Cherokee Nation and a direct descendant of John Ross, Principal Chief of the Cherokee Nation during the infamous Trail of Tears. For more than forty years, Gayle has shared Cherokee stories at schools, libraries, festivals, and performing arts centers throughout the United States. She has authored five critically acclaimed children's books and has appeared in many documentaries, including "We Shall Remain," an *American Experience* episode on PBS. She lives in the heart of the Cherokee Nation in Northeastern Oklahoma. Gayle is also the author of many books for children, including the Cherokee trickster story *How Rabbit Lost His Tail.* Committed to the art of storytelling, Gayle was an early leader in the formation of the Tejas Storytelling Association.

Nazis In Amarillo, TX
Sheila Starks Phillips

I GREW UP IN AMARILLO, TEXAS, DURING THE WAR YEARS. I was six years old in 1940, and war was raging all over the world. Hitler's Nazis were marching across Europe, and the very next year Japan bombed Pearl Harbor. Amarillo was very important to the war effort because not only was there a huge air force base, a Strategic Air Command unit, but there was also a large naval station. And Amarillo Harbor was filled with battleships, PT boats, destroyers, submarines, and even carriers going in and out. Downtown Amarillo was filled with soldiers and sailors looking for something to do with their leisure time. My mama volunteered at the USO, and she often brought young soldiers and sailors home with her for a home-cooked meal. She would receive the sweetest notes from their mamas, who would send little gifts such as an embroidered handkerchief.

It was an emotional time. We were very patriotic and wore our patriotism like a badge of courage. We were proud to be Americans! A number of things went on to get us kids involved in the war effort. For instance, we would take our wagons and go around the neighborhood collecting old newspapers and coat hangers, and we'd haul it all up to the schoolhouse, which was the collection point. We would peel the tinfoil from gum wrappers and make a ball that would grow, and that would become part of our collecting metal. We were proud to be Americans!

Once a week during the school term, the teacher would call us to attention and say, "Boys and girls, put away your books and get out your knitting." For the next hour, we would knit—boys and girls alike. One of the mamas had taught all of us how to knit, and, although it would take us the full term, we would each produce a little six-inch square. Another mama sewed them all together and made a blanket. We shipped it overseas to cover up some wounded soldier or keep a little war orphan warm. We were so proud of that. We were proud to be Americans!

Once a week, we would take our nickels, dimes, and quarters to school to buy savings stamps and savings bonds and dutifully paste them into our stamp books. Once filled, you could turn the stamp book into a bank and receive a war bond. It was my burning desire to be able to buy a $100 war bond at school because when that happened, the teacher made a big production of it. She would call the class to attention and say something like, "Timmy Stewart just bought a $100 war bond." We would leap from our seats, clapping and cheering. And Timmy Stewart would be the hero for the rest of the day. I never got to do that. I don't know if we didn't have the money to buy such a bond or if my Daddy thought I'd lose the money on the way to school, but I never had that moment of glory.

My best friend was a little girl my age named Sara. She lived across the alley from my house. Everyone called her Sara-doo. We looked just alike: two skinny little girls with long stringy mouse-brown hair, gold rim glasses, and a mouth full of braces. We were a couple of beauties. We were each the baby in our families, and that made us special. At least we thought so.

Sara-doo had an older sister named Joanne. We all called her Jopie. Sara-doo and Jopie had two older brothers, ten and twelve years older, and they were both in the Navy. We worried about them all the time. I was particularly worried about Kenneth because I had been in love with Kenneth since I was four- years old. He is the only boy I've ever known who could walk on his hands on the roof of their house. If that doesn't make you special, nothing does.

Sara-doo, Jopie, my two sisters (Pat and Melody), and I made a little gang, and we did everything together. We ran together like a covey of quail. We conducted long debates about whether we would rather be in the Navy, knowing that our ship could be hit by a torpedo. And, if we survived the initial blast and tried to scramble to a lifeboat, we knew a submarine might surface, and we would be riddled with machine gun fire.

81

If, on the other hand, we were in the Air Force, it was likely that we would be hit by anti-aircraft fire. If we were able to parachute out of the burning plane, we would have to hook up with the underground. We knew for sure that we did not want to be in the Army because we would find ourselves in a foxhole with grenades being lobbed at us. We did know that the Marines were the toughest and the strongest because ... Wasn't John Wayne always a Marine?

We went to a lot of movies during those days. Most were war movies. At the intermission, the house lights would come on, and we would stand and sing the *Star Spangled Banner,* and we'd cry because we would have just watched John Wayne battling at Guadalcanal or seen Van Johnson with that cap cocked just so over his eyes get his legs blown off thirty seconds over Tokyo. It was a very emotional time.

We believed with all our hearts that there were enemy spies in Amarillo, and we were constantly on the lookout for them. We didn't worry too much about the Japanese spies because Amarillo, being what it was back then, anyone of Asian heritage would have stuck out like a sore thumb. We were convinced German spies were everywhere. Why, if we saw a car parked too long on a side road, we were absolutely sure it was enemy spies drawing maps, taking pictures, and making diagrams of all the military installations at Amarillo Air Force Base and Amarillo Naval Station. We would ride our bicycles up to the car just as close as we could and try to peek into the windows.

One day, our gang was down at the Walgreens drug store sitting in a booth drinking four hundreds and cherry cokes and blowing the paper off the straws at each other, when we chanced to hear a conversation in the booth right behind us. Jopie heard it first and shushed us. Now Jopie had this wild red hair and freckled face, and she demanded attention, so when she shushed, we got quiet. At first, we could not understand that guttural German accent, but then we realized it was German spies who were planning a second Pearl Harbor. These spies had been in Amarillo for several months and had been taking pictures and gathering information about the military installations, Amarillo Air Force Base, and Amarillo Naval Station. They were to pass on the information to a submarine that was to surface off the beach in three days' time. It was the beach where we always played. With all of that information in enemy hands, a general invasion was planned.

The spies got up to leave, and when they did, we peeked around our booth to get a look at them. They were of medium height, dressed in long, dark overcoats, men's hats pulled down low over their eyes. It just confirmed what we already knew .... enemy spies.

We turned back to each other with our mouths agape. We could not believe what we had heard. We knew if we went to the authorities, or even our parents, no one would believe us. Who is going to believe a story like that from a bunch of six, seven, eight-year-old kids? Nobody!

We knew we'd have to do something ourselves, and so we began to form a plan. Sara-doo took some notes. We felt

83

satisfied that we could manage the situation, so we went home. The next three days were torturous as we were trying to act like everything was A-OK and normal. On the night of the hand-off, we were as nervous as could be. We did not want our parents to get suspicious. My family usually retired early, so by ten o'clock, we were all in bed, and our house was quiet. The next thing I knew, one of my sisters was shaking me awake and whispering, "Get dressed and come on."

We pulled our blue jeans and tee shirts over our pajamas, carried our sneakers in our hands and went tiptoeing down the stairs. We were going to have to pass our parents' bedroom to get out of the house. We did it one at a time. I could hear my mother's even breathing and my daddy's snoring. We let ourselves out of the side door, sat on the steps, pulled on our sneakers, and ran to the alley where we were to meet Sara-doo and Jopie. They were already there. We checked our supplies. Each of us had a Girl Scout flashlight and a rubber gun. Our guns were in the shape of pirates' guns with a spring clothespin attached to the butt of the gun. By hooking cut strips of innertube to the end of the gun and then into the clothespin, when the clothespin was released, the gun would fire. Our mothers were constantly admonishing us, "Don't you point those rubber guns at anyone's face; you'll put their eyes out." After years of playing with rubber guns, we never once put anyone's eyes out.

Once we had checked our equipment, we took off running to the beach where the rendezvous would take place. We knew exactly where it was because we played there all the time. It was one of those nights with a full moon, but it was also cloudy, so it would be bright and then dark, but it didn't matter because we knew exactly where to go. Once we reached the beach, we began to hunker down behind sand dunes and tumbleweeds and waited. It felt like we waited forever, but finally, we heard the tires of an automobile on a gravel road and saw what appeared to be a dark-colored Chevrolet pull up, stop, and turn off the motor. After a few moments, the doors opened. Two men got out and began to walk toward the water. As they got closer, we could see they were the same men we had seen at Walgreens. They wore the same long, dark overcoats and men's hats pulled down low over their eyes. They walked to the edge of the water, just staring out to sea. At exactly twelve midnight, one of the spies pulled a flashlight out of his pocket and began to flash a signal ... blink blink blink ... blink blink. There was a rush of water, and like a giant sea animal, a submarine began rising out of the sea just off the beach. Just then, the moon went behind a cloud, and it got very dark. But by squinting our eyes, we could make out the hatch of the sub opening and two men stepping out and throwing a little rubber dingy boat over the side. They climbed out, got into the boat, and began rowing into shore. When they got to the beach, the two spies pulled them in, shook hands all around, and turned to walk up to the car, where we knew they were handing over all of the information they had gathered.

Once they were some distance away, we went to work.

We ran down to the dingy boat. My sister Pat was the oldest, so she was in charge. She told Sara-doo and me to run to the nearest shore patrol station and tell them what was happening. As we took off running, we could hear what those other girls were doing. They were firing their rubber guns into the bottom of that dingy boat, and we knew it was only a matter of time before it was full of holes.

Sara-doo and I were running as fast as we could with our little skinny legs churning. It was about two miles to the nearest shore patrol station, and by the time we got there, our lungs were bursting, and our legs were giving out. We banged on the door, and when the sailor opened it, we fell into his arms and blurted out the whole story. In a matter of minutes, the whole area was ablaze with searchlights. It was lit up like the middle of the day. We could hear the sirens of the land vehicles going toward that rendezvous area and the PT boats coming from the sea. It was just a matter of minutes until the whole submarine crew and the spies had been gathered up and hauled off to jail. The rest of our gang was picked up and taken to the shore patrol station.

That's when they called our parents. You can imagine how shocked our moms and dads were when they heard what had happened (since they did not know we were even out of the house). At first, they were really mad, and then they were so doggone proud.

The next day the *Amarillo Globe-Times* had a picture of each of us spread across the front page with

86

four-inch headlines that read, KIDS SAVE TEXAS AND THE NATION. And we did, you know.

Sheila Starks Phillips was born in Amarillo and is a proud TCU Horned Frog. Before launching her storytelling career, Sheila worked as a first-grade teacher and a Zookeeper, (similar occupations). A Teller-in-Residence at the International Storytelling Center and featured at the Exchange Place at the National Storytelling Festival, Sheila is a four-time winner of the Houston area Liars' Contest. She is the author of *The Eggstra-Ordinary Surprise,* and several CDs. Photograph by Nesossi Photography.

The Muhindi of Funkytown
DEECEE CORNISH

Terms

Muhind–Used at Kwanzaa celebrations, an ear of corn represents muhundi: the potential of a people for growth and prosperity.

OG–is the term for the founders or original members of a set. (A certain 'hood, or block.)

Shotcaller–the unquestioned decision maker and leader of a set

Triple OG–usually a second-generation gangbanger or a shot-caller with a leadership position

---

IN 1990, I WORKED AT COOKS CHILDREN'S HOSPITAL in Fort Worth, Texas. I was the second shift Dietary Department supervisor responsible for the application of the Fort Worth Independent School District's work-study program. I could recruit kids from Poly Technical High School, Trimble Technical High, and Paul Lawrence Dunbar High School (all three in "the hood"). I supervised teenage boys

88

and girls, from first-year students to seniors.

I got close to four of the boys. Joseph was a junior at Paul Laurence Dunbar. Mandrell was a student at Trimble Technical High School. Theon was a junior at Paschal High School. And "Lil Daddy" was a seventh grader in the Poly Tech Alternative Ed program. They filled a void in my life because I always wanted sons, but God blessed me first with a daughter. Then later in my life came these young African-American teens. I would always talk to them about school on meal breaks, and when we talked about history, I would always incorporate stories of black culture and the things I had seen and in places I'd gone in the military.

We talked a lot about growing up and what it means to be a responsible adult. They got a big kick out of my African proverbs. One of their favorites said, "Do not look where you fell, but look where you slipped."

One day we were in the break room. The TV was playing the evening news. The anniversary of the Little Rock Nine was coming up, so the media was giving it the once over.

Theon asked me, "Mr. DC, what's the big deal with the Little Rock Nine?

"You really want to know?"

"Well, Yea?"

In the back of my mind, I was asking myself, how does he not know this story?

It was a long time ago in a place called America, during an era known as Jim Crow. In 1954, the Supreme Court of

America ruled on *Brown versus the Board of Education.* This was at the beginning of Federal enforcement of school desegregation nationally. The battle for equal rights was hard fought, but we had finally won, or so we thought. Fast forward to 1957, the month of September, in the city of Little Rock, Arkansas. Central High School was set to be integrated. The people involved included nine African-American students under the tutelage and leadership of NAACP chapter leader Daisy Bates and her husband, LC Bates, a newspaper journalist and civil rights activist.

Members of the Little Rock Nine included Ernest Green, Jefferson Thomas, Elizabeth Eckford, Terrence Roberts, Carlotta Walls LaNier, Minijean Brown, Gloria Ray Karlmark, Thelma Mothershed, and Melba Patillo. Ernest was the oldest at seventeen, and Carlotta was the youngest at fourteen. All of them were good students with near-perfect attendance.

When the school opened during September of 1957, the Little Rock Nine were to be the first African-American students to attend Central High School in Little Rock. On September 2, Arkansas Governor Orval Faubus defied a federal court order and stated that he would never integrate the schools in Arkansas. He vowed to deploy the Arkansas National Guard to Central High School to maintain order if necessary.

September 4 was the first day of school for the three boys, Ernest, Terrence, and Jeff. As they walked to school, they were taunted with racial slurs and followed by a mob of young people and adults armed with bricks, bats, and worse. The girls were already at the rendezvous point near the school, along with Ms. Bates and LC. The local police department was doing nothing to stop the barrage of rocks and bottles that the crowd was throwing at the kids.

After a day or so, the story soon began to gain national attention. The Governor dispatched the Arkansas National Guard to maintain "peace," which they did by denying "the Nine" access. The word on the street was that the Guard was there just to "clean up the mess" when the smoke cleared.

After days of abuse, Miss Daisy thought the wise thing to do would be to use her connections in the NAACP to speak directly with President Dwight Eisenhower and ask for help. On September 25, the integrators would try again, but this time with the full support of the White House.

The Nine held regular study sessions at Miss Daisy's home to keep up. They were weeks behind the others in their classes. A messenger arrived from the NAACP office, telling Miss Daisy she needed to get down to the office ASAP. Her departure left the kids with LC. He was working around the kitchen and could tell something was off. There was no playful teasing, no dumb jokes, only blank faces. The kids were scared. They hadn't forgotten the previous experiences or the other attempts. The boys they were "frontin," (to pretend or act like somethin or someone you're not) but they were scared too.

LC called them into the kitchen, offering a snack. On the table, he had a pot of boiling water. In the water was an egg and a potato, and then he sprinkled some coffee grinds in it. He asked them what he was doing and what was happening.

They kind of looked at him like 'duh'?

Smiling, he replied, "You saw me put all three in the hot water; the egg went in all hard on the outside, easily broken, soft and malleable on the inside. Now it's hard on the outside, just like on the inside—and not so easily broken. The potato went in hard and solid, but it came out soft and mushy. The coffee went in, and it didn't change, but it changed the water—making it different, making it better. Here pretty quick, you all are going to be up to your necks in 'hot water.'

You have to decide whether you are going to let the circumstances or the 'hot water' *change you...* Or are you going to change the circumstances? By the time Ms. Daisy returned from the NAACP offices, the kids had gone home. She called most of them and told them that she had talked to the White House and that she had made arrangements for a ride from the United States Army. The best of the 101st Airborne Division would meet them at the school where they would be standing by, having been deployed by President Dwight Eisenhower days earlier.

Throughout the night, the roads to Little Rock were illuminated by the lights of cars traveling for miles to Central High. Meanwhile, near the school, mobs burned effigies on the school grounds. By daybreak, all the streets around Central High were packed with cars, people walking to the scene, or crowding barricades.

Elizabeth Eckford's family didn't have a phone, so she never got word about the group ride on that fateful morning. She dressed and waited for the other kids. And waited. When they didn't show up, she decided that she was going to go on by herself. She mustered up her courage and started walking, holding her books almost like a shield to protect herself. All alone, she walked a gauntlet of racial hatred, threats, and evil.

A crowd followed behind her, screaming, yelling, and calling her some of the most vile things you could imagine. Elizabeth stayed cool even when the angry crowd got so close they could touch her. A *Life* magazine photographer took photos of Elizabeth and the rest of the Nine bravely facing down hatred. He took the iconic picture that's in all our history books today. The Nine rode in the army vehicle.

When they arrived, white kids stood in front of the school. Then came the moment everyone was waiting for. Would the Arkansas National Guard face off with the 101st Airborne?

The Paratroopers of the 101st surrounded the students just as the *stand-down* order was issued to the state guard, which stepped aside and allowed the Little Rock Nine to enter Central High School and history.

I had a copy of the Life magazine cover photo. The next day when my students saw that iconic photo, one of the girls asked, "Mr. DC, who is that?" Pointing at the white girl who was yelling. I told them that the photo was

93

taken on the first day. The girl's name was Hazel Bryan. She didn't even go to Central High School. She came with some friends, driving in from a small town near Little Rock to check out the "action."

As Elizabeth passed their group, they fell in behind her. Hazel, in an effort to prove how cool she was, began to yell louder and be more demonstrative than the rest, working herself into a frenzy. When the photo was released, Hazel became the unofficial national symbol of hate and racism.

That white girl would live a long time and see that image of herself for the rest of her life. I wish this was the time in the story for the 'happy ever' after, but Faubus closed Little Rock schools for the 1958-1959 school year. But they knew a change was gonna come, slowly but surely, one school at a time if need be. Ernest Green would be the first of the nine to graduate from Central High. The change had begun. Change was now in the water.

During the late eighties and early nineties, Fort Worth had a well-deserved and hard-earned reputation. It was known as "Murder Worth" and had twenty-eight active street gangs. The largest of the gangs was VSS Varrio Southside, closely affiliated with the Latin Kings. The 'beef' (fight) reached my kids. One school was red, and the other schools were blue. They asked me, "Mr. DC, have you ever been in a gang?"

"Only if you count the military," I replied. "I don't understand this red and blue thing. You have color lines around your school, right? Well, When I learned about color lines, I was a kid. Color lines were unofficially drawn between black and white communities to separate us and control where we could eat, drink—everything. Now they're drawn between red and blue in our own communities. A long time ago, enslaved Blacks used to call their owners, 'Master.' Now you young people call your masters, 'OG.'"

I continued: "Remember *Kujichagulia,* the second principle from Kwanzaa's self-determination: *When you can't define for yourself who you are, what you want in life, or the path you take, you're a slave.* I ain't never been anybody's slave and I never will be."

I developed rules for the kids in my program: no colors, no 'set trippin'[2], and "save the drama for your mama."

Unfortunately, Mandrell was being pushed into a corner. It was a turf war over a city park. Trimble Tech had been regarded as VSC (Varrio South Central) turf. I started driving my guys home to keep them off the streets and away from bus stops. I kept them safe for about two weeks until one day Mandrell just disappeared. Although it was entirely possible, I refused to think the worst. Ten days later, he popped back up. He had been to "juvie," scooped up by the Fort Worth Police Department while 'beefing' with VSC.

One evening, I made it a point to take him home last so we could talk. He was no longer staying with his cousin. He was now back home with his mom, on neutral ground.

---

2. Any gang violence or rivalry between "sets."

He told me then that he realized he didn't have to be a victim of circumstances. He said he could change them, just like in the story.

"What did you do?" I asked.

"In my Pod at juvie was Polywood Triple OG Fat Cat. He asked me, 'Who do you claim?' I told him I was neutral. Then he said, 'Ain't no neutrals in the hood.' He was taller than you, Mr. DC, but I wasn't scared. I answered OG, Look, I go to tech because it's by the hospital, and I work at the hospital because my mom can't work like she used to. I ain't down, and I ain't scared of you. What's up?"

After lights out, we squared up in the rec room. Polywood Triple OG Fat Cat's crew jumped me. Man, I took a beat down ... Spent three days in the infirmary."

"But you cool now?" I asked.

He replied, "We cool, much respect." I breathed a sigh of relief and thought, *Okay, that's one.*

I never filed any reports, so Mandrell continued to work for me while he was on "paper." When he decided to join the Navy after graduation, I was shocked. I remember his last day. We had a going away party in the break room for him, followed by the saddest drive home—just him and me.

I gave him a prayer card with a Bible verse. "Keep it with you and read it every day." I told him, "My mom did the same thing for me."

Search me, oh Lord, and hold my heart
Try me and know my anxieties

And see if there is any wicked way in me

And lead me in the way everlasting

—Psalms 139: V 13-16

When I got home, I parked in the driveway and had a good cry. The last l heard from him was he had completed Basic training. His people told me that he saw action in the Persian Gulf. I often wondered about him, about all my kids.

In March 2022, at the Texas Library Association conference in Fort Worth, Texas, a young man approached me and said, "Mr DC?"

It was Mandrell, home from the Navy. He had made Chief Petty Officer, trained as a dental hygienist, gone back to school, and earned his master's degree. Now, he was assistant director of procurement at the University of North Texas School of Dentistry in Denton, Texas.

I told him I hardly recognized him with the beard.

He replied, "Well ... You used to have hair." LOL.

Some stories deserve a "Happily ever after" ending.

Deecee Cornish has been telling stories throughout Texas and the country for more than twenty years. He is especially known for his astounding work with at-risk kids. This recognition makes good sense since he is an award-winning performer, educator, and writer known as the "Asphalt Aesop" for his use of folktales, parables, and fables to teach and motivate our children.

Hesitation

BETH TURNER AYERS

HESITATION EMERGED with my daughter's wedding,
a lovely traditional wedding, not far from home.
Then we had a wedding with the groom's family ... in India.

Choosing unique gifts for the family, I thought:
what could be better than something created inch by inch
with them in mind? What could be better than something
held in my hands, hour after hour, color after color?
Two light blues, a dark blue, yellow, just a touch of red.
What could be better than the soft warmth
of a handmade, crocheted, zigzag afghan?
Grasping at the very last stitch,
Hesitation hurled into me with force.
Always lurking nearby, poking, prodding,
making me doubt, Hesitation now *consumed* me.
What was I thinking!? What in the world was I thinking?
Afghans are not needed where mosquito netting is a must,
where windows are open all year, where palm trees flourish.

What was I thinking? Not to mention packing.
This was a bulky bunch of colored yarn ...
my hand-made bulky bunch, so we found room.

I must tell you about Grandfather, the groom's grandfather,
who left his home at the age of seventeen, a refugee
with nothing but the clothes on his back. But he was a visionary.
He could see that hard work and careful planning
could lead him to a home, lead him to family,
to a future when he would be Grandfather, the man of wisdom,
the man with foresight, always the visionary.

The time came to present my bulky bunch of yarn to
Grandfather.
And, let me tell you, Hesitation climbed on that plane with me.
Hesitation crossed the Atlantic, changed planes in Paris,
and followed me out of the Bombay Airport.
Hesitation was nipping at my heels all the way to the very
moment
when I passed the handmade, crocheted, zigzag afghan to
Grandfather
with apologetic recognition that they might not *need* it.

Those visionary eyes lit up. He happily, gratefully accepted this
gift.
Then he vanished. He left the crowded room almost unnoticed,
returned with a plastic bag, a bag he knew where to find,
a bag that had been waiting, sitting in its proper place for
more than fifteen years, yet there was no hesitation
as he ceremoniously placed it in my hands.
I accepted the bag and opened it to see yarn, skeins of yarn.

Yellow, brown, and coral colored yarn ... yarn meant to be held in his wife's hands, meant to flow across *her* fingers as *she* knitted ... something.

There was no hesitation in my acceptance of this tender gift, this heartfelt gift connecting me to his past, connecting me to his grief ... and to his joy. This was a wedding, after all. Grandfather almost winked at me when he told me to make something "Special."
When his visionary eyes met mine, we shared a vision.
We both saw a small handmade, crocheted, zigzag afghan with a touch of yellow, brown, and coral. A soft, warm, blending of our families, to wrap around the future.
There was no hesitation when I said "Yes"
"When the time comes, when the moment is right,
I will make something special." Without any hesitation.

Hesitation worked hard.
That nagging, insistent, relentless Hesitation
almost blocked me from this experience,
almost kept me from finding this connection.
Even now, Hesitation made me pause
before sharing this story, with you.
But there is something you must know about Hesitation,
that poking, prodding, insistent Hesitation ...
Sometimes
you must ignore it.

 **Beth Turner Ayers** is a poet and storyteller. Her poetry covers many topics and appears in anthologies and several other publications. Thanks to her four children, Beth sees the world through the lens of a child. Coupled with her years as a La Leche League Leader, she credits motherhood as the inspiration that drives her poetry. She currently lives in McKinney, Texas with her husband, Mark.

Chocolate Covered Cherries

ELDRENA DOUMA

WHEN I WAS ENTERING MY THIRD-GRADE YEAR OF SCHOOL, I lived with my grandmother and father in a small community called Polacca. It sat at the base of First Mesa on the Hopi Tribal lands in northern Arizona.

My grandma and father were from the Pueblo Tribes of the Tewa and Hopi. We come from the people of the Corn Clan. I was a little girl when the stories of long ago were told of our Pueblo history and how the Tewa came to the land of the Hopi. We heard stories of our traditions, cere-monies, animals, insects, elements of the earth, and how we should act and behave.

Stories of the people were my favorite. I was drawn to stories of the People who lived around us and those who had lived but were now gone. Grandma, my *Siyah,*

103

told stories about her mother, Nampeyo, and her father, Lesou, and how Nampeyo helped in the revival of the Hopi pottery. I knew those stories were especially important because books were written about her, and her pottery is in Museums around the world.

I was told that a day would come when my Siyah and the elders would not be here for those yet to come. For a little girl, that was hard to understand. They said the way our children would learn about their ancestors would be through the stories we chose to tell.

Now fast forward.

Our little family had moved to Amarillo, Texas, and I was getting used to our new community. One day I had to make a quick trip to the grocery store. I made sure I took a list to get only what I needed, which is very unusual for me. As I grabbed a grocery cart and started walking into the store, two women were in front of me. As we walked in together, they spotted a holiday display that was carefully stacked up to greet the customers coming into the store.

I was looking down at my list and didn't notice the display until I heard them complaining about just finishing up Halloween without even celebrating Thanksgiving, and the store was already displaying Christmas items. "Who in the world even buys chocolate-covered cherries anyway," one said. Those words caught my attention.

I did not have chocolate-covered cherries on my list, but after their comments, I grabbed a box from the display, and under my breath, I said, "I do"!

This story I'm about to tell is a story about the time

Siyah, which means "grandma" in our Tewa language, was Mrs. Santa Claus.

It was getting close to Christmas. The missionaries from the church that my dad and Siyah attended were sponsoring their annual Christmas gathering. This was a time when the community would come together, eat, sing Christmas carols, and invite Santa Claus to give out their gifts to the children and other adults in attendance. A pine tree was brought from the mountains far away and decorated by the community. We children, brought paper and popcorn chains and paper ornaments we made at school or in our bible classes.

In years past, someone from the community was asked to be Santa Claus without the children's knowledge. I didn't know this at the time because this was my first year living in Polacca, but my Siyah volunteered when no one else would. In the months leading up to December, I had the chance to get to know Siyah. I experienced my quiet little grandma come alive when we came together with family or at the potlucks our community hosted. She always made the gatherings fun. Oftentimes, when a young man who was our relative would be sitting with his girlfriend at a family meal, Siyah would go over to them, sit on his lap sideways, circle her arms around his neck, and say, "Hello, My boyfriend"! The girl and boy would blush with embarrassment, but everyone else would roar with laughter.

One day while we were eating lunch, a woman missionary visited my grandmother. I called her "Sister K" because she was a Native Hawaiian, and her name was long! She told us that she was having a hard time finding someone to be Santa and asked Siyah if she would volunteer once again. Siyah felt terrible that no one could be found, so she said, "I want others to have a chance to be Santa, so keep asking. Then, if no one is found, I'll do it". What! My Siyah was Santa Claus before. I couldn't believe it. *Boy, I hope they don't find anybody,* I thought.

Close to two weeks went by, and Sister K came to the house to tell Siyah that no one could be found and the Christmas gathering was going to take place in two days. I watched as Siyah started to prepare for the special night.

The next day, she got her empty ten-pound Blue Bird Flour sack out and filled it with clothes she borrowed from my dad—his thermal shirt and pants, a pair of his warm socks, along with her comb. She put everything in her flour sack. When the day came, she asked me to go with her because she might need my help getting ready. That evening it was getting cold, and frost was in the air. She thought we should leave a little early before it became too slippery for her to walk. My dad told me to hold her arm and walk slowly with her. Because we were leaving early, my dad said he still had things to do. He promised to meet us at the church building. We got on our warm coats and gloves, and I waited as Siyah put on her headscarf, then we headed out the door. The church was close to a mile away. I knew it would be hard on her because the last part of our journey would be walking up a hill. But, when Grandma said she would do something, she did it and enjoyed every moment.

When we finally got up to the little church, there was a small turquoise trailer on the south side of the building where the visiting missionaries lived. The missionary living there at the time was Sister K. We were greeted by her and invited into the trailer. She, too, was going to help Siyah get ready. I watched my little old grandma put on her Santa Claus suit. I had never seen my Siyah in pants! She put on Dad's socks and then the black boots. Boots! She always wore black *sneakers.*

Then she let her hair down and asked me to comb it for her. She never let her hair loose! She got her red cheeks ready with a blush. I never saw her with makeup! She stuffed her belly with a bunch of pillows then she practiced her "Ho, Ho, Ho, Merry Christmas"! We told her she looked perfect and sounded just like Santa. She put the beard on last and said, I don't know how men wear beards. They are so itchy!

I knew that people would have difficulty recognizing Siyah underneath that hat, beard, and Santa Claus suit. I was so proud of her as she stood there practicing her "Ho, Ho, Ho, Merry Christmas"! I couldn't wait to see the look on the faces of the people who were already gathering inside the building.

Finally, somebody came to the door and asked if Siyah was ready. As we left the trailer and got closer to the church, we had a surprise coming around the corner from the north side. There before us stood another Santa Claus. As Siyah and the other Santa Claus saw each other, they started laughing.

The people who eventually got their relative to volunteer didn't realize that Siyah was also asked. They said it took them a long time to talk their relative into being Santa Claus. They even found a Santa suit for him and rushed to dress him.

Since there were now two Santas, a decision had to be made to see who would be chosen. I was hoping they would pick Siyah. But I figured they would pick the other because he was a man like Santa Claus.

Then Siyah spoke up and said she would be right back. Sister K and I were motioned to follow her back to the trailer. When we got inside, she quickly removed her beard, moved her pillows from her belly to her chest, and tightened the belt. Suddenly, she had big breasts! We all shared a good laugh.

Then she asked the Sister if she had some lipstick for her lips. She artfully added a little more blush to her cheeks. It was time for Mrs. Santa Claus to gather with Santa and make a grand entrance into the church to give out the gifts. But before they did, Sister K and I went inside. I took my seat, and Sister K told everyone to take their seats because she had heard that some special guests were arriving. Then there was a knock.

As Santa Claus and Mrs. Claus entered, they both yelled out, "Ho, Ho, Ho, Merry Christmas"! As the people turned and looked, they were a little confused because, at first, it looked like there were two Santas. But Siyah was quick and said, "Hello everybody. I'm Mrs. Santa Claus. I had to come and help my husband tonight. He can't see very well nowadays, so I had to drive the reindeer sleigh. That way, he wouldn't get lost. I didn't want to wear my dress tonight because it sure is cold out there. I asked my husband if I could borrow some of his pants. They are a little big on me, but they sure keep my legs warm. Thank you, Honey"! The people couldn't stop laughing. Now I knew why the Sister wanted Siyah to participate in the celebration.

I looked around the room, enjoying the smiles on the people's faces, and the children were so excited. I was proud of what my Siyah had done that night for her community. Her sense of humor made that evening a joy not only for me but for all who attended.

In our family, gifts were not usually given because Siyah and Dad did not have much to offer. I was not expecting one of the wrapped gifts under the Christmas tree that Mr. and Mrs. Santa were passing out. That night I saw my dad get a bag of fruit and ribbon candy, and that made me happy because I knew that was probably all he would receive for Christmas.

Mrs. Santa had one more gift in her hand. She walked over and handed me a little gift-wrapped box. As I took the gift from her, I looked at her with my biggest smile. I opened my gift in front of her. Chocolate-covered cherries—my favorite of all the Christmas treats! I looked up at Mrs. Santa and thanked her. She looked at me and gave me a wink.

After the gift-giving was over, Santa and his wife said goodbye and wished us all a Merry Christmas and Happy New Year!

I still remember that evening walking to the church with Siyah, then taking my place with the other children and receiving that special gift, a box of chocolate-covered cherries.

To this day, when Christmas rolls around, the boxes that hold the dome-shaped chocolate with the cherry surrounded by that sweet syrup that runs down your fingers when you bite into it still beacons from the shelves of the grocery stores.

I'm glad my Siyah gave me so many memories and stories to tell. Especially the night she became Mrs. Santa Claus!

Eldrena Douma grew up in the Pueblo tribes of the Laguna, Tewa, and Hopi. Her cultural background and being a seasoned teacher only served to cement her interest in storytelling. Armed with an appeal for the art of telling, Eldrena intuitively knew that her role as an educator would lead to a life as a professional teller, workshop facilitator, and author. In 2014, she received the prestigious John Henry Faulk Award issued by TSA for her contributions to the art of storytelling. Photo by Katy Pair

The Bicycle Story

Donna Ingham

I SHOULD TELL YOU I COME FROM A FAMILY that has a lot of family sayings. I'll bet you do too. I can go clear back to my great-grandfather on my daddy's side. He was a man of few words, Grandpap was, but when he spoke, he spoke in proverbs.

He lived with my paternal grandparents in Amarillo, Texas, and we would go to Amarillo every year sometime during the Christmas holidays. I remember one year when I was still in elementary school, we were there, and I was out in the front yard of my grandparents' house playing with my boy cousins. For one thing, my boy cousins were nearer my age than my girl cousins, and, besides, I grew up a real tomboy. Well, my boy cousins had learned how to whistle through their teeth, and they taught me how to

111

whistle through my teeth.

I was so proud of my newly acquired skill that I walked into the front room of my grandparents' house practicing. Grandpap was sitting where he always sat in his old oak rocker in front of what we called the fireplace. It wasn't a real fireplace. It was just a mantle with an old open-flame gas stove in it. He sat sideways to it so that he was actually facing the front wall of the house. So when I walked through the front door whistling, he said—as if he were talking to the wall, but this was clearly meant for me: "A whistling girl and a crowing hen will come to no good end."

I quit whistling, at least in front of him.

A Christmas or two later, we were there again, and I got as one of my gifts one of those little autograph books. I was going around asking all the assembled relatives to sign my book. When I got to Grandpap, who I guess was still remembering the whistling episode, because he wrote, "Pretty is as pretty does" and signed it W. W. Davis, just in case I didn't know what his real name was.

Now I'm going to skip a generation because the next sayings I remember came from my parents. My mother would occasionally wax literary when she gave me advice, and she did have good taste. She liked Shakespeare. One of her favorite sayings comes from the play *Hamlet*. It's part of the advice Polonius gives to Laertes before Laertes goes off to France. Even though Polonius is portrayed as a bit of a fool in that play, he does give good advice. He says, "To thine own self be true, and it must follow, as the night the day, thou canst not then be false to any man."

Other times my mother's advice was much more practical and to the point. Especially if I was going on a trip, she would say to me, "Always wear clean underwear because you never know when you might be in a wreck." And she had one sort of all-purpose question that covered a multitude of possible sins. She would just look at me and ask, "What would the neighbors think?"

Now my dad was an old cowboy, so I grew up riding horses. I had a horse before I could even walk, and even before that, my daddy would hold me up in front of him on his horse. If I ever fell off of or got thrown off of one of those horses—which did happen on more than one occasion—my dad would say, "You've got to get back up on the horse that throws you." And so I would.

But when we moved from Brownfield, Texas, where I was born and spent my early growing-up years, to Amarillo, where my grandparents lived, I became something of a city girl. I still had a horse, but I didn't have easy access to her. So, I started riding bicycles

I was in third grade when I got my first bicycle. It was a hand-me-down from my daddy's little sister. This was in the years not long after the end of World War II, so new bicycles were still hard to come by. It was blue, my aunt's bicycle was, but I must have still been thinking of horses, I guess. I was in my palomino period. So, I painted the bicycle yellow with white stripes. I must have ridden that bicycle hundreds of miles in my neighborhood, sometimes "motorizing" it by clothespinning old playing cards on the frame so they flapped in the spokes of the front wheel. The faster I pedaled, the faster my "motor" ran.

I was in seventh grade when I got my first brand-new bicycle. It was green. It was a boy's bicycle because I was still a tomboy. Mostly I wanted the beep-beep horn that was built into the bar that went from the seat to the handlebars.

It would be years and years and *years* later before I got another brand-new bicycle. I was already out of college, working, married, and living in a small-town way up in the Texas Panhandle. My husband and I bought matching Schwinn bicycles, also green. We were in our fitness period. I mounted a basket on the front of my bike and rode it mostly to the grocery store and back.

That was in the 1980s, if I remember correctly. I do remember that, in 2003, my husband and I were invited to visit some good friends in Germany. We were to be there for a month. For the first three weeks, we stayed with our friends in the north and east of Germany, and they toured us around everywhere. I mean, we walked and walked and climbed and walked so that by the time we left and drove south to Bavaria, we were footsore and weary—sort of in our pooped period.

On our first night in Munich, my husband came up from the hotel lobby waving a brochure advertising bicycle tours of the city. Riding instead of walking, we thought. Now that's a good idea.

So the next day, we went down to the train station, where the bicycle rental place was, and signed up for a tour. Our tour guide was a young Australian man named David.

David took one look at us with our gray hair and said, "How long has it been since you rode a bicycle?"

I lied. I didn't mean to lie. I just said the first numbers that came into my head. "Oh, four or five years." Later, when that statistic became more relevant to our situation, I realized it had been more like ten, fifteen, maybe twenty years since we had actually ridden bicycles. Furthermore, I remembered that I learned to ride a bicycle on the flat plains of Texas, where we needed only one speed, and we had those coaster brakes that would stop the bike if we simply stepped backward on the pedals.

Now here we were, climbing aboard twenty-one-speed bicycles with hand brakes. David explained how the gears worked and which brake went to which wheel. I swear I was listening. But my retention was not good that day.

We did fine in downtown Munich because it's flat. And Munich is a very bicycle-friendly city. It has designated bicycle paths. If some errant pedestrian happened to step into that path, all David had to do was ring the bell on his handlebar, and that person would step right out.

Then we got to what I thought was going to be my favorite part of the tour: the ride out along the Isar River on our way to Englischer Garten.

But that's where the hills are.

First, we went up a hill, and I turned the gears the wrong way. It got so difficult for me to pedal that I had to get off and push the bicycle to the top of the hill. David was there to meet me. He was a very tolerant fellow. He reset the gears and said, "That's okay, and besides, now we're going to go downhill."

David headed out first, followed by my husband, Jerry. I was bringing up the rear. It was a long hill and steep. I was watching to see which way David turned when he got to the bottom. That's about when I realized I was going *way too fast.* I was bordering on being out of control. Well, I knew better than to try messing with the gears, so I started squeezing on the hand brakes—both of them. I squeezed harder and harder and harder.

Now, I don't remember the exact moment of impact, but as nearly as we can figure, I either skidded into or simply didn't negotiate the turn at the bottom of the hill. I had managed to slam that bicycle into a fence-like wooden barricade. That pretty effectively stopped the bicycle. But it didn't stop me, and I went flying off the bicycle into that barricade and broke myself. I broke my collarbone, cracked a rib, collapsed a lung, broke my elbow and my little finger, and wound up with a couple of spinal compression fractures. But even then—even then—I knew how lucky I was. I was alive. I wasn't paralyzed. I would heal.

And I was wearing clean underwear.

I spent a week in a German hospital, and then we flew home. A couple of surgeries followed and months of physical therapy. My husband and I bonded in new and totally unexpected ways. He had to help me button, snap, and zip up my clothes. He cut up my food. He was my biggest cheerleader at the physical therapy sessions, and he told everyone his new job was Driving Miss Donna.

The accident happened in August of 2003. As

Christmas approached that year, I was still wearing a back brace, still taking every opportunity to stretch out on the couch with my heating pad, still popping ibuprofen, and still going to physical therapy. But one gift I received that year was truly inspired. It was a shiny, physical testament to my husband's faith that I would soon be one hundred percent well. On that Christmas morning, Jerry gave me a brightly polished, burgundy-colored, twenty-one-speed bicycle with hand brakes. He said to me, "You know what your daddy used to say: 'You've got to get back up on the horse that throws you.'"

And so I have.

Donna Ingham is a retired college professor turned storyteller. She has authored six books and recorded five spoken-word CDs. She's been on the Touring Roster for the Texas Commission on the Arts, is a recipient of TSA's John Henry Faulk Award, and received an ORACLE Regional Excellence Award from National Storytelling Network. She also lies for fun and profit as the Biggest Liar in Texas. Photo by C. Y. Ingham.

Stay out of the Street

JAMES H. FORD, JR.

SEVERAL YEARS AGO, I WAS ASKED TO TELL STORIES in front of a high school class during Black History Month. The person who asked me to tell stories had only heard about story-telling but had not listened to a storyteller tell stories. She questioned me about the type of stories I would tell. My explanation did not solve the problem of getting her to understand oral narratives or family stories. I sent her a tape of one of my performances. After a couple of weeks, I called her to discuss her understanding and whether she wanted to proceed with the performance. She still did not understand what she wanted and what a storytelling performance entailed.

I, too, began to question my style of storytelling. So, I stopped by a bookstore to look at books about black people who have influenced positive black history or who many agree are role models for people of African descent. Upon entering the store, I saw a book on the shelf with a red cover.

The color caught my eye, and I pulled the book from the shelf. Coincidently, the title of the book was *The Red Diary.* It is a 122-year history of black people in Houston and Harris County, Texas. I opened the book and looked immediately at the index section, thinking that by accident, I would find a family member. I looked for Rice and was shocked that on page 164, my uncle was listed as the first black radio station manager in Houston, Texas, at KLVL Radio station in 1949.

As I turned the pages, I found the name Walter Wheatfall. He was the President of the Fidelity Manor High School Student Council in 1958. I flipped forward in the book, looking for 1964 because I was Vice President of the Fidelity Manor High School Student Council. Unfortunately, Dr. Howard Jones, the author of the book, terminated his research on the book in 1959.

I bought the book but decided to continue telling family narratives as I had always done. Sure, telling stories about Martin Luther King, Harriet Tubman, or Sojourner Truth would be nice and could easily be good additions to my storytelling, but they are not the people who have influenced my life the most.

My grandfather was a wonderful storyteller. My uncle C. B. was not only the radio station manager at KLVL but also built an airplane in his front yard, pushed it down the neighborhood's main street, and flew it across the horizon to Houston's only black airport at Sky Ranch. My daddy was my role model.

I remember one Christmas, my parents bought me a Huffy bicycle. That Christmas morning, Daddy put that bicycle together. I couldn't wait for him to put that horn on the side of the mainframe and string those chartreuse streamers from the handlebars. Daddy finally finished, and then he told me to ride on that Bike. I got on the bicycle and headed down to the sidewalk as Daddy walked down to the yard's edge. I looked back, and Daddy lifted his head. I came to a halt. He said, "Hey, boy, you stay out of the street now! You hear me?"

I said yes.

I found out later that the saying "Stay out of the street" was my dad's way of providing me with important principles. He said little phrases like that all the time. "Staying out of the street" was his way of telling me to be careful about with whom I hung out. Watch your surroundings and be respectful of your elders. When I grew older and went on my first date, Dad lifted his head just as I was leaving the door, saying, "Stay out of the street." He meant for me to treat the young lady I was dating appropriately.

When I started thinking about our relationship, I remembered that we spent a lot of time together. On Saturdays, Dad would load his truck with scrap metal, and I would put my saved newspapers in the corner of the truck bed, and we would go to the scrap metal yard and the paper company and sell the stuff to make a few dollars. Then, later, he would go to where his friends were on the corner and hang out for a little while.

I would sit in the truck, drink a Coke, and read a funny book.

When Dad approached the men, they greeted him, and some would say, "Hey Fode, (They never pronounced our name correctly) is that yo boy? He looks just like you. It looks like you spit him out of your mouth." Daddy would smile, and I would smile too." We would smile like my wife says—with a mischievous Ford smile.

I remember the time I heard my Dad's nickname. We were at my aunt's home, and my Dad was seated beside her. Aunt Pat started laughing, and she slapped Daddy on the leg, saying, "Hey, Red, you remember the time you played hooky at school? The next day, momma took your clothes to work with her to keep you from going out into the streets. When she came home that evening, she found you standing with your no-good old friends in front of the store wearing one of my dresses.

I was standing between Dad's legs, drinking a soda. First, I thought about the word *Red.* My daddy was a dark, brown-skinned man. The more I thought about what Aunt Pat said, I remembered when Dad got mad, he did turn a kind of bright brownish-red color. So that day, I turned around and looked at him, smiling when she mentioned him wearing a girl's dress.

I remember when Dad taught me how to garden. He showed me where to put the collard greens and the tomatoes in the garden. When he got tired of digging, he leaned on his shovel. I did the same. I did everything he did. After all, he was the man who spit me out of his mouth.

One time, I went into business for myself. My friends told me I shouldn't do that because my family would suffer. They told me I should keep working and saving money to provide for my family. One day, Dad stopped at my place of business carrying two brown paper bags with two barbeque sandwiches. We sat down at my drawing board and ate those sandwiches. Now and then, we broke out into those sly, mischievous Ford smiles, the ones my wife says we Fords have. When Daddy left, he told me that I should continue to get up early, work hard at my business, and stay late, and I would make it. That was one more of his Fordisms that he told me throughout my young life.

Now I know you think Dad and I always had a good relationship. That is not true. I remember falling out with him so badly that I bagged up my clothes and left home.

I went to my best friend's home, and about an hour later, Dad showed up. He told me I should never tell anyone that he kicked me out of his house because he didn't. He told me that I could stay as long as I needed to stay as long as I abided by his rule. He said that one day, I would have a home, and when he came to my house, he would have to abide by my rules.

I remember once my brother called me on the phone and told me I should come by the house because Dad was having a problem. So, I jumped in my car and drove to the house. When I walked in, I saw Dad sitting on the floor with his back against the couch.

He had beads of sweat rolling down his head. Mom was scurrying around, trying to find clothes before the ambulance arrived. My brother was standing in the corner doing nothing and watching. I went over and kneeled next to Dad. I hugged him.

I started talking to him. I told him about when he got me my first fishing rod, and we fished in Sheldon Reservoir. I told him about when he showed me how to plant a garden. Dad just stared into the distance. Finally, I told him about the time his sister told him about wearing one of her dresses. Dad turned his head, looked up at me, and started smiling. We both smiled. We smiled one of those sly, mischievous Ford smiles, the one my wife says that we Ford's smile.

When I saw him later at the hospital, he stretched his arms out and said, "If it ain't one thing, it's another."

Old James Ford was something extraordinary. Dad was not a Drum Major for Justice. Dad didn't shoot thirty points in an Olympic basketball game. Dad didn't spirit away enslaved people in the underground railroad.

He was the man who walked down to the edge of the yard, lifted his head, and said, "You stay out of the street."

James H. Ford Jr. is a native Houstonian, a professor at Texas Southern University, and very happily married to his wife for fifty-three years. A writer and storyteller, James' signature formula is to thoughtfully blend compassion and humor in his family stories and his tall tales. He combined both genres when telling stories as a young child to keep from getting whipped. He was clearly successful because he was a co-winner at the Houston Storytellers Guild Liars Contest in 1989, and won "Top Liar" in 1990, 1991, and 1992.

The Blow-Dried Cat

A MATTER BETWEEN FRIENDS
JAY STAILEY

THERE ON THE ISLAND OF CLEAR LAKE SHORES, Petee Boudreaux lives year-round in a one-bedroom summer cottage on Juniper Street. Petee's not the oldest person on the island. Capt'n Okie holds that claim to fame. But Petee is easily pushing seventy-five, and feeling pretty good about it, too. Petee's retired now, but for years and years, he trolled a shrimp boat 'round Galveston Bay.

Now Petee is a cat person. You probably know in this world, there are cat people, and there are dog people, and Petee is one of the former. He tried having a dog once, but it just didn't work. He got him one of those retrievers, the ones that are supposed to be good around the water. Petee would take him down to the boat, and the dog would race up and down the pier whining and barking. Then Petee would get him on board, and he'd race around the boat whining and barking. So, he left him up on the dock, and Petee could hear that dog barking and whining until he'd sailed well into the channel and couldn't see the shore anymore. That's one reason why Petee's a cat person. As he's been heard to say, "They don't call 'em 'dog' for nothing!" Cats never acted like dogs when they came on board Petee's shrimp boat. Even though cats hate water, they were good company for Petee once they got on the boat and found a place to get comfortable.

In the last couple of years, when Petee was still shrimping, he had found him a black and white tomcat he named Fisher. Fisher would go with Petee down to the dock every morning, hop on board, and as soon as Petee cranked up that diesel engine, Fisher would jump up on the engine casing and stretch out. That engine would just hum and chug, and old Fisher thought it was purring just for him. And then his nose would start to itch, and he'd stretch out and crank up his own engine. Both engines would purr all over Galveston Bay.

After Petee retired, when the two of them didn't take the rowboat out fishing (Fisher was always awarded the first catch of the day), they could be seen on the front porch of Petee's cottage. Petee would sit in the rocking chair, and Fisher would jump up onto the window air-conditioning unit. When that unit kicked on and started humming, Fisher thought it was purring just for him, and he'd crank up his own little engine, stretch out, and dream he was out trolling on the bay.

Philip Evans lives two doors down and across the street from Petee in one of those big houses built up on stilts. Philip is thirty-eight and works in an upper-level management position for IBM across the lake at Big Blue's regional office. If you had told Philip twenty years ago, when he was a sophomore in college at Youngstown State, that he'd be in upper management with IBM before he was forty, he would have answered you with some sort of obscene gesture. Philip Evans planned to change the world, and he knows you don't do that in upper management at IBM. In fact, Philip is still not real comfortable with just how he got to be where he is at this point in his life. He does know, however, that he has made some decisions before all the facts were in and has guessed right. It's a trait he knows that IBM likes in their upper management people.

Philip Evans is a dog person. You probably know that in this world, there are cat people and dog people, and Philip is one of the latter. Back in Youngstown, the Evans' had dogs long before they had Philip. And after Philip came along, they had more dogs, as far back as Philip can remember. In the Evans family album, there is, it seems, a dog in every picture, at every major occasion in the family history. To Philip, it just seems natural to have a dog. There is something that makes him feel kind of patriotic about going out to walk a dog. So when Philip moved out of his apartment and into the house on Juniper, he got himself a Doberman Pinscher and named him Max.

Now, if you ask Philip if Max is pedigreed, he'll admit he is. "But I didn't bother to get the papers," he's quick to add. And he didn't bother to have Max's ears cropped, or chopped, or blocked, or whatever that is they do to those ears, because he didn't buy Max to show. He just bought him because it's right, somehow, to have a dog.

Petee and Philip are friends. There is something about the manner in which Petee is so comfortable with where he is and where he's been in life that intrigues Philip, and he's hoping that in this friendship, he'll learn some deeper meaning about life. When Philip goes over to Petee's house to sit on the porch and have a beer, he leaves Max chained up in the backyard. Max is not a cat person.

Petee likes Philip all right and is glad for his company. But the thing Petee likes best about Philip is his wife. "Now Marie, she is some girl, and that's fo' sho'," Petee says. Marie is a Lafayette girl and met Philip when he was doing graduate work at LSU. Even though she works in one of those big, tall office buildings in downtown Houston, she hasn't forgotten how to make a great pot of file´ gumbo. Nor has she forgotten about the style of southern hospitality with which she was raised. So, Petee is often invited over to taste those Cajun treats. When he does cross the street to share in some gumbo or crawfish etouffee, Fisher chooses to stay at home. Fisher is not a dog person.

The good news came in November, I recall, of last year. I think it was the second week in the month, when Marie found out that she was pregnant. Philip and Marie had put off starting a family in order to further their careers, but now was the time, and at their little celebration, they invited Petee over and let him know that they wanted him to be the godfather of their baby. I'm telling you, he was delighted with the news, and he couldn't quit talking about it. For the rest of the month, Petee came out of retirement. Every afternoon, instead of sitting on the front porch, he would walk the island. Everyone he met he greeted with a smile and an announcement, "Did you hear de news? Philip and Marie, de gonna have a baby. Fo' sho'! And de want me to be de godfatha'." When he figured he had met up with all his neighbors, he retired, with a sense of satisfaction, back to the porch.

Now, right before Thanksgiving, that same month, Philip once again amazed his bosses by making a decision before all the facts were in, and guessing right. They couldn't quit talking about it. So, they decided to reward him with a long weekend with his wife in Cancun. I've worked in public schools for a number of years and made lots of great decisions but have yet to receive a weekend trip to Cancun as a result of my cleverness. But I understand the private sector sometimes works that way. The happy couple left on the evening of the first Thursday in December, flying out of Hobby Airport on an unseasonably balmy day. They enjoyed themselves thoroughly, and flew back into Hobby on Sunday evening.

When they finally retrieved their luggage and their car and got back on the island, it was well after dark. Marie went on upstairs to bed, exhausted but glowing with memories of the trip and the thought of this wonderful new life to come. Philip had to unpack and tie up a few loose ends before going to bed. He was sitting at the kitchen table checking his e-mail when Max scratched at the back door. He opened the door and looked down, seeing that Max had once again drug home one of his "prizes." In the past, he had brought in raccoons and possums, and once a nutria, one of those big water rats that live in the banks around the lake. Max set the carcass down on the back step, and Philip, not being able to immediately identify it, turned on the light and rolled it over with the toe of his shoe. That's when he realized it was a cat. Bending down to take a closer look, his heart sank. This wasn't just any cat. It was Fisher. Philip put his hands under the little body and carried it into the house. Geez, Fisher was dead alright, stone-cold dead, and caked in mud. Max must have drug that cat all over the neighborhood, probably had it over in the dredging dirt down at the corner of North Shore Drive.

Philip took the kitchen towel and wiped at the fur on Fisher's head, wondering how he would ever be able to tell Petee what Max had done. He kept wiping away at the mud, feeling more and more heartsick. Finally, he just moved the tiny body over into the kitchen sink and, using the dish rinser, washed all of the mud out of the cat's fur. It was then Philip noticed that Max hadn't torn the cat up any, no holes or rips. Philip smoothed out the fur with his hand, and slowly an idea developed in his head. He ran upstairs and got Marie's blow dryer and a comb.

He thought as he blew the fur dry and combed it out, "Maybe if I can just sneak over there, and leave him on the porch, Petee will come out in the morning and find him, and he'll think Fisher just died in his sleep of natural causes."

And that's just what Philip did. He got old Fisher all dried out and brushed clean. Then he chained up Max, and snuck across the street and up onto Petee's porch. He lay Fisher on top of that window AC unit, and kind of stretched him out there like he was dreaming about the bay. Then he snuck back home, swearing to himself that he would not even tell Marie his secret.

The next morning, Marie got up and got herself ready for the drive downtown while Philip fixed them both some pancakes. They ate while they read the paper, and Marie left for work while Philip cleaned up the dishes and had a second cup of coffee. When he went out to get in his car to go to work, he saw Petee Boudreaux standing out on the front porch of the cottage with the couple from the house next door. Philip backed the car out of the driveway, thinking, "Now would be a good time to let myself in on the discovery. I'll stop the car and walk up the steps, and ask, 'What happened?'" So he did. When he got to the top of the porch steps, they were all standing around that window unit, just staring. Poor Petee was shaking his head when Philip said, "Oh, no. What happened?"

Petee just kept shaking his head, and Philip put his hand on Petee's shoulder and repeated his inquiry.

Petee looked at him, just realizing he was there, then shook his head again and said, "I don't know. It sure do beat de hell out of me, I guarantee. Ol' Fisher, he died on Friday, and I buried him dere in de back yard. Dis is strange one, fo' sure. Yep, it sure do beat de hell out of me."

Philip quietly backed down the steps, unnoticed by the little gathering on the porch. He got in his car and drove to work. On the way, he got to thinking about the whole affair, and he reckoned that Petee hadn't quite got it right. Ol' Petee had called it strange. But from where Philip was standing, it wasn't so much strange as it was bizarre. Yep, "Bizarre." That was the word for it. For you see, where Philip came from, it wasn't strange at all for a person to try his best to keep a friend from feeling hurt. He also knew, that when you make your living making decisions before all the facts are in, sooner or later, you're going to guess wrong.

Jay Stailey first appeared as a teller at the 1989 Texas Storytelling Festival. His storytelling journey continued with the Houston Storyteller's Guild. Because his stories often stretch the boundaries of truth, it wasn't surprising when he won two HSG Liar's Contests. He is a past chairperson of the board of the National Storytelling Network, served three years as the Artistic Director of the Texas Storytelling Festival, and was a Storyteller-in-Residence in 2003.

The Fall of the Flies
CAROLINA QUIROGA

BACK WHEN I LIVED IN TEXAS, a land as big as the stories they spin, back when I was looking for what my dad used to call a "serious job" but hoping that the storytelling career would take off, the following happened.

One hot Texas summer morning, as hot as a stolen tamale and so dry that the birds were building their nests out of barbed wire, and after my husband left for work, I went to the kitchen to serve myself a delicious Colombian *cafecito*.

Then I went to the living room, placed the coffee mug on the table, turned the television on, sat on the sofa, and caught the local news reporter talking about the unmerciful heatwave spreading across Texas.

The man said, "Soon, we will be dropping like flies!"

At that moment, I leaned forward to grab my *cafecito* and saw a fly on the rim of the coffee mug. The fly rubbed her upper front legs, scratched the back of her head, and then licked the tip of her upper front legs with delight.

I am telling you, *Colombian coffee is the tastiest coffee in the world!*

Well, I did what most people do, shoo, shoo, and continued with my daily routine. You know: looking for a serious job, walking my dog, eating, reading, cleaning a little, watching TV, and waiting.

As if the fly and I had a gentleman's agreement, we pretty much avoided each other for the rest of the day. That, or she completely disagreed with my taste in loud, upbeat salsa music that I play when I am cleaning the house.

Also, although I opened the back door a couple of times to let my dog go for pee-pees and poo-poos, the fly seemed utterly uninterested in the outside world. Mostly she hung out around the living room.

⌐═══➤

By the next day, I hoped that the fly had realized my relatively poor cooking skills, like that one time when I added a whole cup of salt to the pasta pesto recipe. My dearest ate the meal out of love, but we spent the rest of the night badly dehydrated.

A few days passed, and the fly and I were getting acquainted. I even defended her from my husband when he said, "There is a fly in the house!" As if implying, "You should do something about it!"

But I thought, "Well, what's the harm in having one

fly in the house? She won't last long. She'll soon leave, or she'll die."

At the time, I didn't know that flies could live up to twenty-eight days or more.

Monday, after my husband left for work, when I was having my morning *cafecito* watching the local news, the power went off, PUFF, just when the news reporter was saying ... "Remember, time flies!"

I went outside; the entire neighborhood was without power. And it was while surrounded by an all-encompassing silence that I heard a distinctive humming sound. *Hummmmmmm ...* I thought, *is it outside?* I checked, *nada!*

So, I traced it and located it coming from the biggest window in the house, eighty by seventy inches. I kept its curtains and blinds closed at all times.

I opened the curtain, brought my ear closer to the blinds, and confirmed that the humming sound was coming from the other side. I was perplexed. I had been rewatching the X-files, and many crazy theories were running through my head. I paired them up with a dream my mother had the other day about being abducted by aliens. As many witnesses have reported, there is always a humming sound preceding an abduction.

Since everything is possible in Texas, I gathered my courage, twisted the wand, and as the blinds opened, they revealed the most incredible yet frightening scene. Hundreds of flies lived a busy life between the blinds and the window glass. I am talking about baby flies, toddlers, and adolescent flies going through a phase, young adult and adventurous flies, parent flies, middle-aged flies going through a crisis, beggar flies, and even grandma and grandpa flies. I mean, the whole society was right there. Now, if you are not yet impressed, let me tell you what I found to be the most remarkable, they had created a perfect replica of an old Western town.

Oh yeah! I saw a general store, a saloon, a schoolhouse, a bank, a sheriff's office, a gunsmith's building, blacksmith stables, a hotel, a land office, dry goods, and a clothing store, a telegraph office, a stagecoach depot, and apartments for the cowboys' flies and their families.

I could tell the saloon was open because I saw two dizzy flies come out holding on to each other, laughing, and then falling on the floor in a stupor! Then I saw the sheriff, the biggest of all the flies, with a well-trimmed mustache. He was outside, watching an unfolding duel between two male flies that had gotten into a buzzing argument over a very coquettish lady fly who was terribly unsure who she should love forever. Their quarrel captured the attention of the other flies. They came out to watch, and placed a bet or two.

The suitors counted to ten and walked away from each other. Then they turned around, pulled out their guns, and fired away, *pew, pew!* After the suitors had canceled each other, the very coquettish lady fly, bored with the outcome, went back to her life. All the other flies did, too.

As if I was the fly on the wall, I continued watching this freaky marvel of nature. That is when I heard caskets as if someone was riding horses. So, I directed my attention about five inches southwest of the town, likely five miles in human distance. That is when I saw a band of six bandit flies riding roaches that were chasing Western music. They were being chased and shot at by another group of flies riding small lizards. The lizards were also chasing Western music. There were several casualties, but I could not tell who the good guys were.

Finally, I saw what seemed to be a very serious old male fly going back and forth to the main street, shouting and preaching, "The First Mother Fly has brought us all to the promised land. Thus, it remains our duty ... No, no, no, it remains our cultural destiny to grow, populate, and expand beyond the deserted borders of our native window."

I thought, *Ah, how curious; history tends to repeat itself even on such a tiny scale. Cute.*

With shock and disbelief, I closed the blinds, thinking my husband was going to totally, irretrievably ...

Then, a disturbingly paranoid thought began to take shape in my head. *What if those flies listened to that old male fly prophet and decided to take over mi casa, my house?* By the time my husband returned home, my dog and I would be food for maggots. Oh no! Not on my watch. I was about to get busy, busy as a stump-tailed bull in fly season.

Perhaps it was that, in Texas, people are bold, which could be contagious. So, I went to my closet and put on the pink Texan boots a dear friend gave me when I left Tennessee for the Lone Star State. I adjusted my bandana, grabbed a belt, and tied two grocery bags around it—they looked like gun holsters. Lastly, I wore the cowboy hat I bought at a party store last Halloween. But still, I needed my weapon of choice. So, I went into the kitchen, pulled out the top right drawer, and grabbed the *blue trapito*—the dark, ragged remains of a favorite kitchen towel. It was the towel my mama had sent me from Colombia. It had been in the family for generations. Its history spans over five hundred years, perhaps more in a different story.

Legend tells me that my *blue trapito* was used to wipe the tears of *La Llorona,* She is the weeping woman who goes around crying and frightening people from Mexico to *La Patagonia.* Her tears are said to be so powerful that they can resuscitate *los muertos (*raise the dead). My *blue trapito* has endured extremes of hot and cold, turmoil, unrest, revolutions, the fall of dynasties, hurricanes, floods, and all the bloody Colombian wars. So, there was no doubt that my *blue trapito* could take down some unwelcome buzzing insects nesting *en mi casa,* my house.

Armed with my weapon of choice, I went back to the living room, ready to unleash the most severe punishment on those *forajidas* (outlaws). It is hard to describe the thirst for cold fly blood. It was a throbbing, vengeful desire in my heart. I had had enough. I had been kind to the lone lady, but she had taken it too far. I was not going to have on my hands another Alamo. *No, señor!* We were paying a mortgage!

There was only one solution; get rid of them all!

Now, I will pause here because I can hear some of your thoughts, wondering why I didn't use a fly swatter—or an insect spray. An aerosol bomb sounded more efficient, and they cover more territory. Well, had I used one of those, I wouldn't be telling this story. Also, I didn't have any of those boring tools *en mi casa!* So, moving on. It was eleven o'clock in the morning! The job was going to take me all day. So, *manos a la obra,* let's get to it, I said.

So, I walked towards the window, swinging my *blue trapito* in the air, and it looked as if I was going to lasso a steer. Then I twisted the wand and pulled the cord all the way down. The blinds went all the way up. And right there, I began swinging my *blue trapito* from side to side, from left to right, like a whip. I took them by surprise. Well, just at first, because soon I realized that those cowboy flies were not going down easily.

To my amazement, they began pulling out their guns, pistols, and rifles and started to shoot at me. *Pew! Pew! Pew! Ouch! Come on, guys! That hurts!* It stung ... a little, like a pinch. After I recovered from being attacked, I realized that their bullets were made of roach poop, which was gross, yet left me unharmed.

Despite the tiny holes their bullets made in my shirt—which I had to burn afterward—I continued swinging my *trapito,* from side to side, from left to right for hours. One by one, they surrendered and fell numb on the windowsill. I picked them up as they fell and bagged them for sanitary reasons.

By the time my dearest returned from work around dusk, I was proud of a good day's work. With humble pride, I threw my hat over the windmill. Now, I had two bags full of stunned flies. Saying nothing to my partner, I tied the bags and left them in the garage, awaiting their sentence to be decided at dawn.

The next morning, I took the bags to the backyard. I held them up so they could hear me loud and clear when I said: "You have greatly annoyed me, but you have done what nature tells you to do: grow and expand. Even we humans continue to do it at the expense of others. You do not deserve to die by my hand. But I do not want to ever see you *en mi casa* again." So, I put the bags down, untied them, and watched them fly fearfully away.

But that is not the end of the story.

Next summer, a fly "accidentally" wandered into *mi casa*. And when we happened to coincide in the same space, I came closer and said: "Have you heard the story, *The Fall of The Flies?* Do you know who I am?"

She looked at me with her compound eyes; then she broke into a sweat. A tear rolled down one of her eyes, and with a shaky voice, she asked: "Bzzz ... Are you the one with a whipping *blue trapito* that caused the fall of first fly town? Bzz"

The one and only. *Esa soy yo!"* I said.

"Bzzz, Oh! Please have mercy!" the fly implored.

"Fine! But at your earliest convenience, please fly to the back door. I will open it, and you had better get out because, as they say, around these parts, don't mess with *mi casa!*"

She did as I said.

Oh! I know the story of my legendary deed has spread far and wide across the insect kingdom. Some have even exaggerated the tale. You know how it is when you mix time, fear, imagination, and a storyteller or two. Some have said that my dog was the one who single-handedly accomplished the whole feat. Others have said I am twelve feet tall and have three heads and eight arms! How else was I going to bring them down to their knees? They say that I am as mean as a mama wasp, that my *blue trapito* is faster than double-struck lighting, and that my swing is so strong that I make Samson look sheepish and sensitive.

Well, I don't care how they spin the yarn, because I learned a thing or two. I learned that storytelling is my serious job and that stories are so powerful that they can ignite, grow, expand, and even cause the fall of civilizations nesting in a window or on a lonely planet. So my friends, if this story isn't a fact, then God is a possum!

Carolina Quiroga was born and raised in Cali, Columbia. She is a bilingual storyteller, performer, and podcaster. Her performance background, combined with a master's in Storytelling from East Tennessee State, has helped her build an impressive repertoire of bilingual stories which explore myths, legends, folktales, and historical narratives of Latin America and Hispanic cultures. Carolina has performed at festivals, conferences, and venues throughout the country and has educated and entranced diverse audiences at numerous schools, libraries, and colleges.

Ferbigated Catholic

SUE KUENTZ, ED.D.

MOM AND DAD RAISED US FOUR KIDS AS METHODISTS, attending Sunday School when it was available, church on Sundays when possible, and we always looked forward to the monthly pot-luck dinners. Dad was an Air Force pilot, which made us kids "military brats." My family moved about every three years to posts all over the world until I turned thirteen. We lived in Germany, Turkey, Japan, Hawaii, and eventually made our last family move to San Antonio, Texas. Depending on whether we lived on base or off base, if we weren't close to a Methodist church, we'd visit a Baptist church or a Lutheran church. I was captivated to witness some baptisms in the Baptist church when a grown man or woman would be dunked in what seemed to be a small pool! Visiting the Lutheran Church, we had fun trying to figure out how to use the typed song verses in the church program and match the words to the music on the designated hymnal page. We failed miserably at that. It wasn't until we lived in Japan in the mid-1960s that I realized there might be more to religion than I thought!

I was eight years old and called Susy when we settled in at our quadruplex at the American Compound in Kanto Mura, Japan. As a military brat, you learned to make friends fast. My new friend, Suzanne, lived next door to me, while my other new friend, Cathy, lived at the end of this quadruplex. We three were all about the same age, so it was great to get out in the courtyard after school to play tag, hide-and-go-seek, and four square until our parents called us in for dinner each night. The weekends were even better because we'd take turns spending the night at each other's homes. It was one of those nights when I realized what I had been missing!

We were upstairs in Cathy's bedroom when she and Suzanne showed me the glittering new necklaces they received from their church. Each piece had its own unique beauty. One was a strand with petite white pearls and what seemed like tiny diamonds that glistened in the overhead light, while the other was made of what looked like rubies and blue sapphires. The girls exclaimed that I could only receive one myself if I were Catholic. At that moment, I didn't know much about being Catholic, but if that meant receiving a priceless necklace like theirs, I was all in!

With that revelation, I couldn't waste another second. After saying my goodbyes, I grabbed my overnight bag and rushed back over to my house, just in time for Mom's spaghetti dinner. Even though no one was expecting me, I sat down promptly, folded my hands, and chimed in with our dinner prayer *God is great. God is good. Let us thank him for our food. Amen.* I believed in that prayer more than ever! Smiling at my parents and siblings, I proudly announced that I wanted to become a Catholic.

Mom and Dad briefly looked at me, and both simultaneously said "No," without missing a beat while placing their twirled spaghetti on a fork into their mouths. Mom saw my disappointed face and added, "Susy, we're Methodist and would like to remain Methodist. We know you might have your reasons, but our minds aren't changing— you're Methodist."

I did the only thing a hot-headed girl could do— screeched my chair out, stood up, and dramatically stomped my feet upstairs to my bedroom. That didn't change their minds. But, in time, I figured I could convince my parents otherwise.

Two months later, my mother's parents, Grandma and Grandpa Hennings, flew over to Japan to visit us for about two weeks. They were both educators, as was my mom, so it was an opportunity for them to see how the elementary school functioned on the Air Force Base as well as visit some Japanese schools off-base. About midway into their visit, Mom drove Grandpa and the rest of us to Chofu Elementary School, where Mom taught third-grade science while we were in grades from first through fifth. This was a huge elementary school that housed fifteen hundred students on

144

three floors.

The car ride to school in our VW van seemed typical at first. My sister, two brothers, and I were talking and arguing over this or that while Mom and Grandpa carried on their own conversation upfront. In the midst of all the chatter, my ears were keen on Grandpa's voice. I distinctly heard Grandpa tell Mom that he received the great honor of becoming a Ferbigated Catholic. STOP THE PRESSES! Yep, you heard me right. My Grandpa was a FERBIGATED Catholic! Not just a normal Catholic. He was a FERBI-GATED Catholic. My eight-year-old brain quickly racked up all the benefits of this new knowledge. I immediately deduced that Susy Berg was not only Methodist but given the honorary title of being a Ferbigated Catholic since a grand title such as Ferbigated Catholic must trickle down to the grandkids. And, because I was now a Ferbigated Catholic, I could choose the best of the best of those necklaces that Suzanne and Cathy had received. *Hmmm, opals and diamonds would be nice on my chosen necklace!*

I was popcorn in the pan excited and couldn't wait to tell my friends at school the great news. Mom parked the van on the black tarmac in front of the school's office, and we jumped out to have a few minutes to play with our classmates before the bell rang to line up. I figured by the time the school bell rang, half the school knew about my new title, thanks to my big mouth. In fact, after the Pledge of Allegiance and the morning announcements in the classroom, Chofu Elementary's principal came on the intercom asking if Susy Berg could please report immediately to

145

Mrs. Berg's classroom. I was beaming! Maybe there was going to be a big celebration in my mom's classroom.

I rushed out of the room and up the ramp to the third level and scampered quickly to Mom's science room. Grandpa and Mom were waiting for me outside her door, and their faces looked stern and severe. Mom immediately bent down to meet me eye to eye, nose to nose, and said, "Susy, the entire school seems to be talking about you becoming something like a Ferby-something Catholic! What in the world is that all about, young lady?"

Grandpa was standing tall with his hands on his hips, waiting for my answer, while Mom stood up and joined him with her arms crisscrossed around each other.

I enthusiastically looked at both of them and responded, "Isn't it cool that we are Ferbigated Catholics because Grandpa was made one?! I can't wait to pick out my own gorgeous necklace, like Suzanne and Cathy have, only better!"

Mom and Grandpa looked at each other, puzzled, so I quickly added for clarification, "Don't you remember Grandpa? In the van this morning, you were talking to Mom about becoming a Ferbigated Catholic."

Grandpa thought for a moment, and a light seemed to switch on in his head. A huge, understanding smile crossed his face while he placed one hand on my mom's shoulder.

He turned to her and said, "Ann, I think I understand what Susy's talking about. Let me have a chat with her, please." Grandpa bent down on one knee so he could be on my level.

146

"You remember that, Grandpa?" I asked.

Grandpa responded, "I do remember talking to your mom in the car, Susy. It was pretty loud where you were sitting, so I'm surprised you heard anything in the front seats! I believe you thought you heard that I became a Ferbigated Catholic, but that's not what I told your mother."

"What *did* you say, Grandpa?" I asked nervously.

Grandpa continued, "Susy, I actually exclaimed to your mother that I was honored to be inducted into the Phi Beta Kappa—a national academic honor society. I'm afraid you misunderstood the words that came out of my mouth. I'm not a Ferbigated Catholic."

Looking at Grandpa and then up at Mom, taking all this in, I realized that I wouldn't be receiving a necklace anytime soon, and I had a lot of explaining to do with my friends.

Years later, I was living in San Antonio and sharing this same story with my middle school storytelling students. One of the girls pulled out of her jean's back pocket, a plastic Rosary with a little explanation book and gave it to me, saying, "Thank goodness there's no such thing as a Ferbigated Catholic."

I agreed!

 **Sue Kuentz, Ed.D** tells stories that encourage listeners to tap into their own childhood, including tales about the funniest and scariest moments living abroad as an Air Force Brat. Her signature warm and animated style is also perfect for the collection of multicultural folktales, fairytales, urban legends, and personal narratives she delivers to the families in her audiences. Sue is on the Texas Commission on the Arts Touring Roster, recipient of the 2016 Tejas Storytelling Association's Colson-Herndon Storytelling in Education Award, and the 2023 John Henry Falk Award recipient.

Uncle Uno's Knife

LOREN NIEMI

WHEN I WAS A CHILD LIVING IN HIBBING, my family would go to my grandmother's farm on weekends. My father would help milk the cows or butcher chickens.

It was a small dairy farm a few miles outside town, with a solid square house set on a little rise, a red barn (big enough for a dozen cows) down the slope next to a pond, and scattered in between an outhouse, a garage, the chicken coop, and—since we are Finns—the holy of holies, the sauna. Beyond the outhouse was a small grove of crab apple trees and, next to it, a fence with almost forty acres of rocky soil on the other side that was reserved for hay.

Because we are Finns, we would take saunas. It was our traditional culture and a social community experience. Families would come to spend a little time in the sauna and

149

visit my grandmother. They came and went all through the day.

My father would say it was for our health as he marched my brother and myself down to the sauna, past the dreaded rooster who liked to flap his wings, squawk, and rush at us to peck our legs. It was a terrifying journey to learn the rites of cultural identity.

When we arrived at the already warmed shed, we would take off our clothes in the small changing room, hang them on a peg, and enter the semi-darkened space of the sauna itself. Inside, it had a stove with a bed of rocks on top, a bucket of well water, a tin dipper, and three cedar benches, each set a foot or so above the other. Fire, water, steam, soap, and rinse was the order of the day. We were too young to roll in the snow or plunge into the farm pond, though I was told the adults would once darkness fell.

Afterward, my parents would eat fresh baked bread or sweet rolls with coffee in my grandmother's kitchen.

Mostly I remember the heat of the kitchen and the smells of coffee perking and cinnamon rolls baking, stews simmering in big black pots or thin dark stacks of pancakes hot off the griddle covered with butter and maple syrup. The smell of kerosene, the smell of bacon cooking in cast iron skillets, of anise seed, of fresh milk still warm from the cow: all would make appearances. In my memory, the farm was always rich with scents and bathed in the golden light of Grandmother's smile. I recall sitting at the table, gazing at her face as round as the full moon with a babushka, sipping coffee that she sweetened by the sugar cube she clenched between her teeth. "Boyka," she would say, holding me on her lap, "Sumalina boyka" which roughly translated as "Finnish boy."

This one time, when I was five or maybe just turning six, my uncle Uno appeared at the door, and he motioned to me to follow him. I left my mother and Grandmother in the kitchen and followed him into the living room, past the table with the lace runner and the open bible, past the green horsehair couch and my dead grandfather's chair that I had never seen anybody sit in. Into the hallway and up the stairs to the second story, each corner occupied by small bedrooms I had never been in. Up the creaky stairs leading to the attic, where he lived, with the slanted walls marking the roof and the brick chimney marking the center of the room.

There was one electric light hanging by the door, barely illuminating the room despite the best efforts of the bare bulb. Across from the door was his narrow bed, and along the walls, his clothes hung on nails. The wedding and funeral suit hung on the furthest nail, the Sunday shirt next to it, and then the progression of worn overalls and woolen shirts, long underwear, and jackets in various states of clean to dirty marching towards the door and the laundry thereafter.

This, too, was a world of smells. Sweat, manure, wet cotton, musty woolen blankets, the single bottle of Old Spice he reserved for those weddings and funerals sitting on top of his dresser next to a comb and shaving mirror.

My uncle was a small man. For many years I thought

of him as a gnomish figure, tousle-haired, watery eyes, and a toothless grin, hunched over. Now I realize that if I had spent a good portion of my life in a room where the only place one could stand straight was in the center, I might be stooped as well. And it was to that center he went, to the dresser that seemed too big to have ever fit through the door or come up the narrow stairs.

"Open your hand," he said and held his out, palm up, to show me how. I did so. He opened the top drawer of the dresser. He pulled out something and turned to fix me in a solemn gaze. "Every Finn should carry a knife at all times," he told me in a hushed whisper as he placed a small jackknife in my outstretched hand. "Don't tell your mother!" he cautioned as he closed my fingers around the brown handle of the small, two-bladed knife.

But the admonition, "Don't tell your mother!" was unheard. My entire attention was focused on the knife. *I had a knife.* I was a Finnish boy with a knife. A two-bladed knife. In my eyes, that knife might as well have been a sword. As I went back down the stairs, I could not take my eyes off the knife. With every step, my heart swelled with pride. I had a knife. I was a Finnish man!

Without a moment's hesitation, I marched into the kitchen, thrust out my hand, and declared that I had a knife. Without a moment's hesitation, my mother snatched it away. I couldn't believe it; my knife was gone. It was gone. Vanished. I burst into tears and turned to run to my uncle Uno.

"What's done is done. I told you not to show it to your

mother. Come, we will go outside and feed the chickens." In my disappointment, I did not even care if the rooster was there.

A few years ago, we were sitting around the table telling stories, and I told that one. My mother got up and left the room. I thought I had upset her, but when she came back in, she said, "Hold out your hand." When I did, she put a small jackknife into my waiting palm. "You're old enough for this now."

It was the same knife, the small, brown, two-bladed knife my Uncle Uno had given me thirty years earlier.

The farm is gone now. The forty acres were sold to our second cousins to expand their dairy operation. The house, the barn, the sauna, and the sheds were demolished to make way for the new highway. My grandmother is gone now. She worked the place until she was eighty-three, then fell and broke her hip. Died in a rehab center soon after. My uncle Uno is gone now. Shook himself to death with Parkinson's disease long ago. All gone. Dead and gone. But I still have the knife, and when I hold it in my hand, when I tell the story, they are with me still.

 **Loren Niemi** began as a child fibber but soon realized he was less interested in lying than he was in improving the truth. He is still at it, as an author, poet, and innovative storyteller of philosophically and emotionally complex traditional and original stories. His legacy includes a 44-year history of performing for audiences of all ages. He was the 2016 recipient of the National Storytelling Network's Lifetime Achievement Award. Photo by JoAnn Niemi.

Duty

Tim Couch

THE BEAM OF THE POLICE OFFICER'S FLASHLIGHT sliced through the stygian night beneath the bridge spanning the Trinity River. He and his partner were only doing their duty. They had to move along with the homeless, the destitute, the mentally ill, the drunk, and the druggies, who, by their presence, diminished downtown Dallas. That was their responsibility, at least according to the elected representatives of the city council.

The officer strode from one huddled figure to another, forcing them to consciousness and stumbling movement. Then he came to one smaller than the others. And, when that teenage boy awoke to sight of the blue uniform, he began to cry. The officer, who had a son about the same age, forgot his assigned duty. He motioned his partner on, sat on the concrete abutment, and began to talk. The story the policeman heard spilling out was a familiar old tale of anger and incomprehension, of youthful rebellion and stiff-necked parental authority. One night, poisonous words like "I hate you" and "I wish you were dead" were spat at a father.

Murder was not the resulting offense. Instead, in the dead of night, the father's wallet and car were purloined. From Saint Louis, Missouri, the boy sped south and westward. At first, he used the credit cards freely until he realized the charges revealed his location. So, he sold them in a back room for easy cash.

By the time he reached Dallas, Texas, that cash was gone. The car was sold on the street to someone who didn't worry about a title or ask any questions. Soon, that money, too, was gone. It wasn't far from there to life under the bridge.

Duty did not impel the officer to direct the young man to his patrol car. He simply told his partner they had someplace to go. And he drove to the Children's Emergency Night Shelter on Harry Hines Boulevard. There, he was told by a weary Child Welfare caseworker, that there was no bed available. There weren't enough beds for the child abuse victims in the small shelter, so there certainly was not a bed for a teenage runaway and thief.

The policeman looked the boy in the eye and said there was another option, but it required him to take responsibility for his actions. The boy was ready to do that. So, they drove to the building next door.

I was just doing my duty the next morning when I reported to the Dallas Juvenile Detention Center. I, as a recently hired Assistant District Attorney, was reporting for detention hearings. A detention hearing determined who stayed in the juvenile jail and who went home. With limited space in the Detention Center, most went home unless they were too dangerous or unless their parents refused to take them.

I showed my freshly printed photo identification card and was buzzed through the first heavy steel electronic door. In a small anteroom, I opened my leather briefcase to demonstrate that I had no weapons or contraband. I was then buzzed through a second steel door and admitted to the Center.

Through all the years I was an Assistant District Attorney, I never became accustomed to the clang of those doors slamming shut behind me.

I settled into the District Attorney's office behind reinforced glass. The glass was embedded with chicken wire so it wouldn't shatter if struck by a thrown chair or a human body. My job began with reading the police reports on those who had been arrested the previous day. I had just finished an arrest report about a runaway car thief from Saint Louis when Mr. Lee, a probation officer, appeared and asked if he could use my telephone. The phones in the probation officer's office and the District Attorney's office were the only ones near the courtroom from which long-distance calls could be made. I agreed and saw a gaunt, hollow-eyed boy enter the office and begin to dial. "Dad, it's Jim.

I'm in Dallas, Texas. I'm sorry, Dad. Sorry for everything. Can I come home?"

There was a pause. Then he lowered the phone, wiped his eyes with the back of his hand, and addressed Mr. Lee. "He wouldn't even talk to me." I remember that was an easy hearing before the judge. There was no parent. The boy was detained.

The next morning, I reported to the Juvenile Detention Center again, just doing my duty. On the folding chairs in the waiting room for the court, directly outside my office, a couple of people caught my eye. There was an older man hunched over. He looked exhausted, and his skin was like aged parchment about to crumble, betraying too many late nights consuming only coffee and cigarettes. Beside him was a fellow who looked like he was playing college football. He was big and handsome, but his lips were a slash of anger. In small courtrooms, attorneys quickly learn to pay attention to angry people.

About the time I was starting to get worried, they brought in the prisoners. When the older man unfolded from the chair, I saw where the college boy got his size. With a cry, the large man embraced the boy who had used my office telephone yesterday.

Mr. Lee materialized at my door, a grin on his face. "That's the dad. I called him later. He wasn't mad. He got so choked with emotion when he heard his son's voice, he couldn't say anything. He drove all night with his other son, just to be here for the hearing this morning. Jim hung up too soon."

That was when I did something beyond my duty, something I wouldn't have done if I had been a more experienced Assistant District Attorney. I went and sat beside the young man, who I now knew was an older brother. I introduced myself as the prosecutor. "Based on what I see, I don't imagine that you'll be pressing theft charges. So, your brother will be released to come home."

The older brother's eyes blazed. "As far as I'm concerned, you can bury him under the jail. You can't imagine all he has put Dad through." Then that handsome face softened. "But look. Look at how happy Dad is." "My Dad," he said, shaking his head. "My Dad not only will ask for his release, but he'll probably let Jim drive our new car on the way back home. That's my Dad."

Tim Couch practiced law for fourteen years before transitioning to a career teaching religion to middle school students and leading chapel services at the Episcopal School of Dallas. He retired in 2017. Tim received the John Henry Faulk Award from the Tejas Storytelling Association in 2022. Be sure to have Tim tell stories at your next Halloween party. Once, while telling ghost stories to his students, a boy jumped up and said: "That's it. I'm out of here."

Miss Ellen, The Baby Lady

Toni Simmons

MANY TIMES, WE HEAR ABOUT PEOPLE WHO ARE FAMOUS all over the world. Here is a story about someone who was a treasure in her own community.

"Miss Ellen! Miss Ellen! Come quick! The baby's coming! The baby's coming."

That was the call Miss Ellen Sturrup heard many times. People all over Coconut Grove came calling for her whenever someone was in labor because: (You can sing this part!)

She was the baby lady, baby lady.
She was the baby lady, baby lady.
She was the baby lady, baby lady.
She was the midwife.

Yes, Miss Ellen was the midwife in Coconut Grove for thirty-five years, and she delivered hundreds of babies—or, as the folks would say—she "brought them into this world."

That was the way it was, especially in the black communities of Miami-Dade County, Florida. These were the days of segregation. Black patients were segregated in city hospitals to dilapidated, unclean, and generally undesirable areas of the hospitals. Because of this racism and the unavailability of doctors, most black women preferred their own midwives. Someone they could trust. Someone they could depend on. Someone like Miss Ellen because:

> *She was the baby lady, baby lady.*
> *She was the baby lady, baby lady.*
> *She was the baby lady, baby lady.*
> *She was the midwife.*

During this time, Bahamians immigrated to Miami. Many settled in the Coconut Grove area and brought with them their own midwives, their own remedies, and their own healing styles. Miss Ellen came to Miami in 1910 from the Bahamas. She had been trained by her mother, Charlotte, who was part Cherokee.

Miss Ellen was a pretty woman with fair skin. She had long black hair that she wore pinned up in a bun with big hairpins. Don't mistake her prettiness for softness. She was known to get anybody straight. Miss Ellen rode a bicycle with a big wooden basket in front. When going on her deliveries, she would carry hot water, a little black bag, and food in the basket. She always took something for the family to eat because there was sometimes no food in the house. She carried the hot water with her because often there was no indoor plumbing, and you would have to wait for someone to get the water and for the water to be heated. Miss Ellen would visit her patients for nine days or more after the delivery, making sure things were right with the babies and mothers. Miss Ellen never failed to take the families food. Miss Ellen loved her work, and the families loved her because:

She was the baby lady, baby lady.
She was the baby lady, baby lady.
She was the baby lady, baby lady.
She was the midwife.

One day, Miss Ellen sent for her mother, Charlotte Ingraham, from the Bahamas. They both worked in Coconut Grove and South Miami as midwives. Miss Charlotte would walk in her white starched apron, going to anyone who called. She carried a black bag too. Sometimes she and Miss Ellen went together. There were times that they stayed hours into the night waiting for the delivery.

In 1931, Miss Ellen delivered her first set of twins. It was June 22, and Miss Maggie, the mother, had gone to work that day. She worked as a housekeeper, which was known as "day work." Late that night, she went into labor. Someone came running for Miss Ellen.

Miss Ellen jumped on her bike and rode two blocks to Charles Avenue. She delivered the first baby. It was a girl, about five or six pounds. She waited and waited for the placenta to come. An hour and forty-five minutes later, she noticed there was not a placenta but another baby coming. This time, it was a boy who only weighed about three pounds.

The people in the room were silent, almost holding their breath. They thought the second baby was stillborn. Someone even called for the mortician. Then finally, the tiny baby cried. They put the babies in a dresser drawer. Miss Ellen and Miss Charlotte often taught their patients to make cribs out of boxes or drawers. Miss Ellen had also delivered a set of triplets once. Nothing was too much for her because:

> *She was the baby lady, baby lady.*
> *She was the baby lady, baby lady.*
> *She was the baby lady, baby lady.*
> *She was the midwife.*

Now you've often heard about fathers being nervous during labor, about them panicking or even fainting. Miss Ellen had a patient whose husband got so excited that he ran out of the house and locked the door behind him with his wife inside. He ran down the street hollering. When Miss Ellen arrived, she could hear the mother screaming. She had to get someone to break down the door. She got inside in time and delivered the baby.

Even though Miss Ellen's patients loved her, the white doctors weren't too happy about having the midwives around. One doctor said, "When a woman is in her neediest time, she is often at the mercy of some coarse old dame or ignorant black granny." Another doctor called them a "necessary evil" to be controlled and regulated. Regulation meant required education, licensing, and, very likely, elimination. The state sent nurses to teach, train, and instruct midwives on state standards. They organized midwives' clubs that met monthly. Miss Ellen served as president of one of the clubs. Midwifery was transformed from a moral, social custom to a newly-regulated service, somewhat like nursing. But that wasn't all.

After licensing, there were regulations, guidelines, and many rules to be followed. Filing birth certificates was one. The certificates had to be perfect—no errors permitted. The recording was done by hand. Miss Ellen's daughter, Verneka, did the recording on the certificates for her mother's patients. When midwives tried to file the birth certificate, administrators would always try to find some mistake, however insignificant.

Miss Ellen was no pushover. I could hear her thick Bahamian accent now, insisting on saying, "It t'aint so." Difficulties with the health department didn't stop Miss Ellen, though.

Miss Ellen continued her practice until 1966. Even though she didn't pass on her gift to her daughter, she was allowed to be in the delivery room of the hospital when her daughter delivered her baby. And that baby was me. Talking 'bout ...

She was the baby lady, baby lady.
She was the baby lady, baby lady.
She was the baby lady, baby lady.
She was the midwife.

My grandmother, Ellen Sturrup.

Toni Simmons' interactive tales have captivated audiences throughout the U.S. and around the world. She has performed at the National Storytelling Festival Exchange Place and the National Black Storytelling Festival. She was designated as an American Masterpiece by the National Endowment for the Arts and is a recipient of both the Tejas Storytelling Association's John Henry Faulk Award and the National Storytelling Network Oracle Award. Photo by Rex Nash.

Little Gladys and Fireman Lux
A TRUE STORY
PIPPA WHITE

I've got a story about a hero,
A totally forgotten one, too;
My story takes place in 1907,
And please keep in mind, it's true.

1907 near Seward, Nebraska,
A sweet September day.
The Dixon children were ready for school,
Isabel, Robert, and Tray.

Off they went over the fields,
While Baby Gladys trailed behind.
Baby Gladys was nineteen months old now,
And her curly blond hair just shined.

But she couldn't keep up with the others,
Yet she wasn't ready to return to home.
The day was so soft and warm.
It was a day to explore, to roam.

Gladys saw pretty wildflowers:
Pink and yellow and blue.
She saw fences and cows and cornfields,
The perfect prairie view.

We know children attune to Nature;
Gladys rejoiced in the earth and the sky—
In the sunshine, the warmth, the beauty,
And all those lovely things that could fly.

What should she look at next?
So much to offer, this great, big world—
The grass, the breeze, the expanse,
All new to such a little girl.

And then Gladys spied the train tracks,
Straight and narrow and strong.
She could walk between those tracks,
Like a path, who knows for how long?

So this was her special place then,
This path of wood and steel,
Stretching so far in each direction,
Why it hardly seemed quite real.

Now Gladys had heard train whistles.
Gladys had heard that rumbling sound.
She knew what locomotives looked like.
Oh, my, what had she found?

Because staring down the tracks, she saw the engine.
She knew what to do. She waved!
She smiled, and she jumped, and she squealed.
That's how you were supposed to behave.

That poor engineer tried to stop the train,
Knowing, of course, too late!
Every engineer's worst nightmare,
And now that nightmare would be his fate.

But also on board was Fireman Lux,
And Fireman Lux saw that child, too.
He got out on the footboard, then the cowcatcher,
He'd have only one chance, he knew.

He sprang from the cowcatcher and, while in midair,
He grabbed little Gladys, little Gladys so fair,
My story is true. This is not a tall tale,
They rolled down the embankment, both hearty and hale.

Mrs. Dixon had heard the train whistle,
And when she did, her heart had leapt.
Where, oh where, was Gladys?
"Oh, no, not that!" she wept.

Out of the house she ran in a panic,
"Please keep my baby from harm!"
Walking towards her was Fireman Lux,
With Baby Gladys on his arm.

The dictionary definition of hero,
Well, it's too long to be included here,
"Valor, bravery, achievement,
Courage over fear."

But those people who know, "my chance may be nil."
But they dare anyway; they risk it still,
They push themselves out on the slimmest of limbs
As if staring down death was just an everyday whim.

Their names fade too quickly,
We forget them, that's true;
Noble, courageous people
And ordinary as me and you.

So all I can say is, "Thanks, Fireman Lux,
Because when my life is a challenge, when my world is in flux,
I can think of people like you, and know that all is not lost,
And that maybe I can dare, too, dare whatever the cost."

Pippa White transitioned to storytelling after a career in theatre and television. In fact, her "One's Company Productions" is part theatre, storytelling, and history and can best be described as history laced with inspiration. Pippa has entertained and inspired audiences at universities, performing arts centers, museums, and festivals in over thirty states.

The Osage Diamond Ring

FRAN STALLINGS

CHARLIE O'DONALD WAS A SMART, good-looking young man who didn't like to get his hands dirty. He had seen enough mud in the trenches of France fighting in The Great War, and he figured a fellow could parlay his wits and looks into an easy living. New Orleans suited him fine, especially when the 1920s started to roar. So, he wasn't all that interested when his old Army buddy, Bill, came back from the Osage country in Oklahoma, all excited by what he had seen.

"They're pumping money out of the ground," said Bill. "They've struck oil in the Osage, and the money is running like water. New buildings are going up all over Pawhuska: mansions, skyscrapers five and even six stories high! Electric streetlights, big cars! Those Osage Indians have so much money, they hardly know how to spend it. I

170

figure we could help them some ..."

Charlie didn't see the appeal of a raw new prairie state. "Indians in blankets and feathers?"

"No, Charlie, you got that wrong. Those old Osage families, they send their sons to Harvard and their girls to finishing schools in France. When the girls come back, they can *par lay vu fran say* just as good as those *dee mo zels* we saw in Paris. Bobbed hair with a Marcel wave, high heels and silk stockings, dresses in the latest French fashion—so short you can see their knees!"

The girls got Charlie's attention. But he frowned at the black grit around Bill's fingernails. "So, we would buy up some land and drill for oil?"

"No, you can't buy it. The whole county is in allotments: back in '06, the federal government shut down the reservation, and each of the Osages who were on the books, two thousand or so, got one headright. Drillers can lease it, but it belongs to the Indians. And here's the thing, Charlie: all the income from the leases, and ten percent of the oil sales, goes to the whole tribe. Every headright gets an even share."

"Then it must not amount to much for each one."

"Are you kidding? Last year, in 1921, each headright got over $10,000. (By the way, in 2024 dollars, that's almost a million.) And some Osages have more than one, like if they inherited headrights from their parents or their husband."

Inherited? Now Charlie was even more interested.

"So, you want to go into the dry goods business? Sell silk stockings and stuff?"

"Noooo, Charlie! I saw all those Pierce Arrow touring cars and those Stutz Bearcats they were driving, and I remembered what we learned when we were in the Army motor pool: cars break down! We could open a mechanic shop."

But Charlie wasn't listening. He already had an idea of his own.

Closing out his schemes in New Orleans took several weeks. Charlie called in debts, sold things he didn't need, and had a couple of suits tailor-made—not too somber, but not flashy either. New shirts, new shoes, and a new hat in the latest style. Soft silk neckties, just a bit colorful. He bought a one-way train ticket to Pawhuska, set aside expense money, and then spent all the rest—every thin dime, every red cent—on a diamond engagement ring.

For folks nowadays, diamond engagement rings are standard, but in the 1920's that fad was just starting. Before then, any kind of ring would do. And Charlie wanted the latest fashion.

As the train rolled into Osage County, Charlie saw oil well derricks thick as porcupine quills on those sorry Flint Hills. Coming into town, he saw the tall buildings, the shiny shop fronts, the big cars—and the pretty Osage girls, just like Bill said.

Charlie settled in carefully. He went to mass at Immaculate Conception Catholic Church up on the hill, already famous for its imported stained-glass windows.

172

He attended music concerts at the Constantine Theater—but not the moving pictures or the vaudeville shows (too lowbrow). He mixed with only the best people. And he met Maggie Runninghorse.

Maggie was the only child of a prosperous and respected Osage widower, who was not happy when Charlie politely asked permission to pay court. But Maggie begged—this stranger from New Orleans was so dashing, so cultured, so cosmopolitan! His elegant clothes and manicured nails reminded her of Parisian gentlemen. Papa Runninghorse sensed something amiss, but he relented.

Charlie took Maggie to concerts and programs at the library. The young couple was invited to salon evenings at the best houses. Maggie was so proud to be seen on his arm! And he doted on her, writing poems and bringing flowers. At mass, he got permission to sit in the Runninghorse family pew.

Papa scowled when the young couple asked for his blessing on their engagement. That night, he demanded the ring from Maggie, and, the next day, drove into Bartlesville to have it tested. "I think it's glass," he told the jeweler.

But the jeweler examined the gem under his magnifier and found no flaw. He used it to scratch a pane of glass, then a plate of steel. "This is a genuine diamond, all right." And so, Papa Runninghorse grudgingly gave his consent, hoping that if the ring was on the level, Charlie was too.

Papa's wedding gift was a new house for the couple. Not one of the stone and brick mansions you can still see on Grandview Avenue, he thought a modest three-story frame

Victorian would do for starters. But it had all the modern amenities: indoor plumbing, electric lights, even one of those new mechanical refrigerators! Maggie spent happy weeks decorating and furnishing it.

In fact, they held the wedding reception in that house to show it off. All the important town folks came, and all their Osage clan members, too, including Maggie's cousin, Elaine. "Poor orphan," Maggie explained, "she lost her brothers, sister, and parents in the Spanish influenza. The nuns raised her and then sent her overseas. She's just come home to Fairfax. Be nice to her!"

Charlie did some mental arithmetic. Two brothers, sister, and parents: Elaine had at least *five* headrights in addition to her own! Charlie vowed to be *very* nice to Maggie's cousin, Elaine.

The newlyweds lived happily, taking part in Pawhuska's social life. But after a few months, Maggie began to complain of digestive troubles. The town ladies nodded knowingly: she must be "in a family way." But her clan aunties were puzzled by the fact that Maggie didn't wake up with morning sickness. Indeed, her nausea and vomiting didn't start until about an hour after breakfast.

Concerned that she wasn't eating enough, her doting husband insisted on preparing her meals himself. He brought her delicate poached eggs on toast and a cup of the bitter chicory coffee he had learned to brew in New Orleans. She loved drinking it French style, half and half with hot milk. Even when she couldn't manage a bite of breakfast, she'd drink a cup of Charlie's bitter coffee. But within the hour, even that would come up.

Lunch was no better, and she often had no appetite for supper. The clan aunties fretted: an expectant mother should be round and rosy, but Maggie became thinner and paler each day. Her beautiful black hair fell out by the handful.

Barely six months after her spring wedding, Maggie lay in her casket. The undertaker had done an excellent job with wig and paint: she was still beautiful in her favorite pale silk dress. The guests were arriving, and there was Cousin Elaine! Charlie looked down at Maggie's hands folded on her breast and realized she was still wearing that diamond engagement ring. Oh no! He was going to need it for Elaine!

Charlie thought fast and fell to his knees in a paroxysm of grief. He threw himself on the corpse. "My darling!! I can't bear to be without you!" Hidden by his body, his hands quickly slid the ring off her emaciated finger. He hid it in his fist!

Papa Runninghorse tapped him on the shoulder. "Control yourself, my boy. The priest is here." Charlie straightened up and saw a hand extending from a lacy cassock sleeve.

But he couldn't shake it. He had the ring in his right hand, and sticking it in a pocket first would look suspicious. Instead, he covered his face with both hands and moaned, "My darling is gone!" Then he hunched over sobbing, loud enough to cover the GULP as he swallowed the ring.

"There there," said the priest, "it will pass."

Yes, it will, thought Charlie. I'll be very careful.

~T~

That evening, a wild thunderstorm took out the electric power. Charlie brought a kerosene lamp up to the bedroom and tried to relax with a glass of brandy, but in the wind, he seemed to hear a faint voice in the distance: *"Give me back my diamond ring."*

Nonsense. He tried to concentrate on his plans. How soon would it be proper to pay court to Cousin Elaine?

He turned down the lamp and stretched out alone in the big bed. Think of the future!

Wind fluttered the curtains at the open window. They reached out to him like ghostly arms. *"Give me back my diamond ring."*

He sat up and lit an expensive cigar to calm himself, but with each inhale, its glow in the darkened room seemed to reveal a pale figure reaching out to him, approaching... *"Give me back my diamond ring."* It came closer.

His nerves broke! He leaped from bed, overturning the lamp and dropping his cigar in the spilled kerosene.

~T~

They found his bones in the ashes of the fire that destroyed the house.

No one has rebuilt in that spot. Sometimes sightseers come to pick through the ruins, although all that's left standing is the rock chimney amidst the rubble.

But some folks say that if you go out there on a moonless night when there's just a bit of breeze, you may hear the wind moaning around that chimney.

It sounds like, *"Now ... I've ... GOT!! my diamond ring."*

NOTES

I originally contrived this story in 2010 for a ghost walk in my hometown, Bartlesville, Oklahoma. Although some of the venues actually had reported ghost sightings, I was assigned to a jewelry store with no such history. I searched for a folktale about a haunted gem but found nothing! However, I had heard about the notorious murders in neighboring Osage County, and *The Osage Indian Murders: The True Story of a 21-Murder Plot to Inherit the Head-rights of Wealthy Osage Tribe Members* (by former FBI agent Laurence J, Hogan, 1998) filled in gruesome details. I proceeded from there, incorporating motifs from my favorite jump tales.

To my amazement, a ghost walk attendee from Pawhuska told me afterward, "I know where those ruins are! Nobody has built there yet!"

My 2010 fictional story became more relevant with the 2017 publication of David Grann's best-seller *Killers of the Flower Moon: The Osage Murders and the Birth of the FBI*, recently made into a major motion picture.

 **Fran Stallings, Ph.D.,** tells traditional and original stories both in North America and abroad. Her repertoire also includes unique environmental "folk-fact" tales and Japanese folktales, which she collected with educator and author Hiroko Fujita. Along with her companion, the mouse puppet she always keeps in her purse, Fran is that teller who is ready in an emergency to enchant any listener who happens to come her way. She is a recipient of TSA's John Henry Faulk Award and two ORACLEs from the National Storytelling Network. She lives in Bartlesville, OK. Find Fran online at www.franstallings. com. Photo by Mark Blumer.

The Lion Cub and the Goats
GENE & PEGGY HELMICK-RICHARDSON

WE CREATED THIS STORY after hearing the renowned mythologist Joseph Campbell share a much-abbreviated version. When we couldn't find a full account of this folktale, we decided to write our own. Over time, we made changes to suit our style of telling and who we intended to tell it to. (And isn't that what "folk" tales are all about?) We have found this story to be popular with teen and adult audiences and especially well-received in settings such as drug and alcohol treatment centers and prisons.

Although the version we have provided here is how we perform it in our two voices, the story can certainly be told by a solo teller. Our suggestion for telling: when the lion cub "speaks," give him a goat accent.

179

THE STORY

Teller 1: A drought had fallen on the land, and it had not rained in over a year.

Teller 2: The rivers stopped flowing.

Teller 1: The watering holes turned into mud wallows.

Teller 2: The grass turned brown, dried up, and blew away.

Teller 1: The animals began to leave this area by ones...

Teller 2: Twos ...

Teller 1: Tens ...

Teller 2: Twenties ...

Teller 1: Hundreds ...

Teller 2: And thousands ...

Teller 1: The only animals that stayed behind were those who were too old and sick to travel, and they were just waiting to die.

Teller 2: There was one exception, though, and this was a young lioness. The only reason she had stayed behind was because she was pregnant, too big to travel.

Teller 1: She was waiting to deliver her cub, and once it was strong enough to walk beside her, she planned on the two of them leaving the area together.

Teller 2: But as the days passed, it grew harder and harder for her to find food.

Teller 1: One morning, the lioness woke up and realized that, because of the strange feelings in her body, her cub would be coming that day. She was afraid because it had been three days since she had eaten anything.

Teller 2: So the lioness began to walk across the dry,

180

hard, cracked earth to search for food.

Teller 1: She lifted her head and listened as the wind blew past her ears.

Teller 2: Then she raised her nose and sniffed the air.

Teller 1: Oh, there was no doubt about it—goats were nearby!

Teller 2: So the lioness walked to a cliff that overlooked a small valley.

Teller 1: From that cliff, she looked down into the valley and, to her amazement, there she saw a spring bubbling up.

Teller 2: Around the spring was a pond.

Teller 1: Around the pond was a patch of grass.

Teller 2: And feeding on that grass was a small herd of goats.

Teller 1: The lioness knew all she had to do was leap into the valley and catch a goat. Then, she would have a fine meal that would give her the strength to deliver her cub. She just hoped that she had the strength to survive the jump.

Teller 2: So with what little energy she had left in her body, the lioness jumped off the cliff, and she landed with a splat.

Teller 1: The goats fled in terror.

Teller 2: When the goats returned to their beautiful green valley a few hours later, they discovered to their horror, that there in the middle of it now laid a dead lioness.

Teller 1: But curled up next to the lioness was a lion cub, and it was still alive!

Teller 2: The goats began to argue about what they should do with the lion cub. Finally, after a great deal of debate, it was decided that they would raise the lion cub as one of their own.

Teller 1: So they began to pass the lion cub from mother goat to mother goat, and these mother goats took turns nursing it. On that nourishing goat milk, the cub grew strong and healthy.

Teller 2: Soon, the cub grew too strong and too healthy, and finally, the day came when the cub was too big to nurse. When that happened, the mother goats pushed the cub away and taught him to eat the grass like their little kids.

Teller 1: Soon, the cub stopped growing.

Teller 2: He quickly began to lose weight.

Teller 1: His fur started to fall out.

Teller 2: His ribs began to stick out.

Teller 1: His nose was hard and dry.

Teller 2: His tongue was swollen.

Teller 1: His paws cracked and bled with every step he took.

Teller 2: Anyone who looked upon the lion cub could tell he was dying, but the goats never said a word.

Teller 1: By this time, the drought had come to an end.

Teller 2: The rivers began to flow.

Teller 1: The mud wallows turned back into watering holes.

Teller 2: The grass grew strong and green.

Teller 1: The animals began to return to this area by ones ...

Teller 2: Twos ...

Teller 1: Tens...

Teller 2: Twenties ...

Teller 1: Hundreds...

Teller 2: And thousands.

Teller 1: One afternoon, a magnificent and stately lion returned to the area.

Teller 2: He had not eaten anything that day and decided it was time for another meal.

Teller 1: So he lifted his head and listened as the wind blew past his ears.

Teller 2: He raised his nose and sniffed the air.

Teller 1: Oh, there was no doubt about it—there were goats nearby!

Teller 2: The lion walked to the edge of a cliff that overlooked a small valley.

Teller 1: From that cliff, he looked down into the valley, and to his amazement, there he saw a spring bubbling up.

Teller 2: Around the spring was a pond.

Teller 1: Around the pond was a patch of grass.

Teller 2: And feeding on that grass was a small herd of goats.

Teller 1: The lion knew that all he had to do was jump down into that valley, and he would catch himself a fine meal.

Teller 2: So he sprang off the boulder and landed in the valley. The goats fled in terror.

Teller 1: But the lion didn't care because he caught a goat when he landed.

183

Teller 2: But when the lion lifted his paw to view the meal he was going to enjoy, instead of a goat, he saw a sickly, scrawny, pathetic-looking lion cub.

Teller 1: "Boy! What are you doing here?!" he roared.

Teller 2: The cub just looked up at him pitifully. "Baaa"

Teller 1: "Don't you talk to me like that! You're not a goat, you're a lion, and lions roar! Give me a roar, boy!"

Teller 2: But the lion cub just shook his head. "Gooooat."

Teller 1: The lion was losing his patience. So he nudged the cub up to the side of the pond and took his big paw, and pushed the cub's head down, forcing him to look at his reflection in the water. Then the lion put his head next to the cub's so their two reflections were side by side. Then he roared, "Look at your reflection, and then look at mine. There is no denying that you are pretty pitiful-looking. But there is also no denying that you look more like me than those goats you've been living with. You are a lion!"

Teller 2: But the cub just shook his head again. "Gooooat"

Teller 1: Now, the lion took a few steps back and looked carefully at the lion cub. He could tell the cub was dying. Then he got to thinking about who he found the cub with. The lion put two and two together and figured out what had been going on, and he was mad! If he didn't help the poor little cub, who would? So the lion picked the cub up by the scruff of the neck and carried him up to a nearby cave. He dropped the lion cub at the entrance to the cave and demanded, "Don't move. I'll be back in a minute!" And then he took off.

Teller 2: The poor little cub was so terrified and so weak, he did just that. He stayed right where the lion had dropped him.

Teller 1: A few moments later, the lion returned, dragging the carcass of a freshly killed gazelle. He dropped his prey in front of the cub and started pulling off hunks of gazelle meat and eating them. After a few mouthfuls, the lion tore off a hunk of gazelle meat and held it out to the lion cub.

Teller 2: But the lion cub was disgusted. He just shook his head and declared, "Graaaaass."

Teller 1: The lion roared, "No! Goats eat grass; lions eat meat. You are a lion, so you must eat the meat. You will die if you don't eat the meat!"

Teller 2: Once again, the lion cub shook his head. "Gooooat! Graaaass!"

Teller 1: The lion lost it. He reached over, grabbed the lion cub, and pried his mouth open. Then, the lion took the hunk of gazelle meat and forced it into the cub's mouth. Then he clamped the cub's mouth shut and held it shut ...

Teller 2: ... until the cub finally gave up and swallowed.

Teller 1: Then the lion let go and watched the little cub.

Teller 2: The lion cub glared at the lion. But after a few moments, he spoke, "Moooore?"

Teller 1: "Sure," said the lion, and he ripped off a hunk of the gazelle meat and handed it to the cub.

Teller 2: After that, the cub pulled off his own hunks of meat.

Teller 1: And when the cub was full, the lion finished his meal. When he was done, the older lion announced to the cub, "Now let me show you something else lions do really well—nap!" And he stepped out of the cave and into the sunlight. There, he stretched out on the warm grass and closed his eyes.

Teller 2: The cub, his belly now full, stretched out next to the lion and closed his eyes.

Teller 1: The lion turned to the cub and said, "Today, you have had your first lesson in being the lion that you truly are."

Teller 2: The lion cub's eyes popped open. He then looked up at the old lion and proclaimed, "Rooooar."

Gene and Peggy Helmick-Richardson share the stage as "Twice Upon a Time Storytellers." They deliver a range of stories, often in tandem, to audiences of all ages. Their repertoire includes traditional stories, personal narratives, and historical re-enactments. "Twice Upon a Time..." was selected to perform at the 2005 National Storytelling Regional Concert in Oklahoma City and as featured storytellers at both the 2010 Texas Storytelling Conference and the 2019 Texas Storytelling Festival. They were also on the Texas Commission on the Arts Touring Artists Roster for over fifteen years. Both Gene and Peggy were recipients of the John Henry Faulk Award and jointly received the Marvin Brown Volunteer Service Award. Photo by John Lehman.

A Little Seed of Truth

DARCI TUCKER

I LOVE STORIES ABOUT ORDINARY PEOPLE who do extraordinary things. Texas is full of those stories—stories of legendary people who did legendary things. The historian in me always wonders how much of the legend is true. I mean, I'm sure that there's a little seed of truth in each of those legends, but what was that seed? How did the legend start?

I actually watched a seed grow in my own life.

As a young child, I had serious allergies and asthma. I was pale and painfully skinny—my kneecaps stuck out like snow globes. My favorite sport was a spell-a-thon. I was a teacher's pet who was well-behaved and always did my best work. When I was five years old, my hair was cut in a pixie: short in the back, over the ears, sideburns, bangs, with a bow on top of my head for picture day. I was a nerd.

We moved to a new town just before I started first grade, and I was nervous about starting a new school. The other kids already knew each other from kindergarten, and I wanted to fit in. I agonized over what to wear. I picked my red plaid dress. Should I wear the bow on my head? Should I not? I went with the bow.

Only two other girls wore dresses on the first day, and I was the only one wearing a bow.

Then I saw Bernetta Thrasher. Unlike me, she was burly and athletic.-She had scabs on her knees and wore a permanent scowl. She would stalk into class in the morning, slam her lunch box into the cupboard, and smile if she heard the glass in somebody else's thermos break. She was mean. She was the kind of kid who'd trip you as you walked past her desk. She'd steal your homework. And believe it or not, she lived on Golden Rule Lane. Really.

My parents were fond of quoting what my mom called the Thumper Rule from the movie *Bambi:* "If you can't say something nice, don't say anything at all." This left me woefully unprepared to deal with someone like Bernetta. Mom said the best thing to do was just to stay away from her.

That worked fairly well until November, when my school, like many schools back then, had a Thanksgiving pageant. Some of the classes would portray Pilgrims, and some of the classes would portray Indians. My class got to portray Indians! I was so excited! I had a cousin with brown eyes and long black hair who was the most beautiful girl I'd ever seen. I thought she looked just like an Indian, and now

I was going to look like an Indian, too!

On the Monday before the pageant, a man from the local market came and dropped a big pile of burlap potato bags on the floor. The bags would be our costumes. They were tan and floppy, kind of like buckskin, and you could pull out threads to create fringe. They were perfect! But the minute he dropped them, a cloud of dust rose into the air—and I began wheezing and sneezing. I was so allergic to the burlap that I couldn't stay in the classroom. So all that day and the next, while the other kids fringed their burlap and made construction paper headbands with colorful construction paper feathers, I sat alone in the library.

At the Thanksgiving pageant on Wednesday, my classmates sat resplendent in their burlap bags. And way down at the end of the risers, away from all of the other kids, I sat—in a brown paper grocery bag.

You've watched *Animal Planet* and *Mutual of Omaha's Wild Kingdom.* You know what happens when strong animals see weak ones. Bernetta attacked. She began rubbing her eyes, making wheezing sounds, and taunting me, "Boo hoo! My eyes are so itchy!" And that was just the start.

Throughout the rest of elementary school, she called me names, stole my lunch money, let the air out of my bicycle tires, and made the game of dodgeball into a nightmare. I'd be in the center of the circle thinking, *Please don't hit me! Please don't hit me!* And WHAM! The ball would hit me in the head.

"Bernetta dear, please don't aim at their heads," the teacher would say.

"I didn't mean to," Bernetta would smirk, before WHAM! She hit me again. "Sorry, teacher."

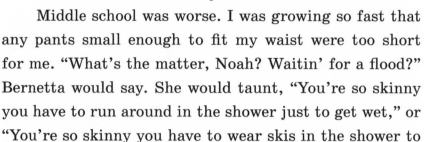

Middle school was worse. I was growing so fast that any pants small enough to fit my waist were too short for me. "What's the matter, Noah? Waitin' for a flood?" Bernetta would say. She would taunt, "You're so skinny you have to run around in the shower just to get wet," or "You're so skinny you have to wear skis in the shower to keep from going down the drain," or "You're so skinny that if you turn sideways, you disappear, which is fine, because nobody wants to see you anyway."

One day in seventh grade, it looked like my luck was finally changing. The phone rang, and it was Todd! Heart-throb Todd, the cutest boy in my class! He was calling to ask if I wanted to go ice skating!

I put my hand over the receiver and called out, "Mom! Mom! It's Todd! He wants me to go ice skating with him tonight! Yeah, I know it's a school night, but—but Mom, it's TODD!! Mom, PLEEEEEASE!!!"

"Sorry, Todd, I can't. It's a school night." Click.

"MOM, YOU'RE RUINING MY LIFE!!!"

The next day as I walked into art class, Bernetta and Todd were talking and laughing. When I got to my seat, they stopped. After a few minutes, I leaned toward Todd and quietly said, "I'm sorry I couldn't go skating with you last night."

"I didn't ask you to go skating," he scoffed. "I wouldn't go skating with YOU!"

He winked at Bernetta, who practically shouted, "Darci thought YOU would go out with HER?? Haha-haha!!" The whole class turned and looked at me. The blood pounded in my ears. I wished I was dead.

Several months later, during PE, we were playing basketball. As usual, it was the big, burly girls against us little, wimpy girls. Bernetta had been fouling me, and fouling me, and fouling me. And then she fouled me again. I took a deep breath to try to calm my rage, and stepped out of bounds with the ball to pass it back to one of my teammates. Before I knew what I was doing, I slammed the ball as hard as I could at Bernetta. It hit her in the head.

Just then the bell rang, and I ran.

I ran as fast as I could.

My mind was racing.

I couldn't get on Bus twenty-four.

We both rode Bus twenty-four.

If I got on the Bus twenty-four, Bernetta would beat me up. Or she would wait until I got off the bus and beat me up then.

She'd follow me off the bus and beat me up, and there would be no one there to help me.

I couldn't get on the bus.

And then I saw Barbara. Barbara didn't ride Bus twenty-four.

Barbara rode Bus seventeen.

I grabbed her arm and said "I'm coming home with you today,"

And she said "Okay,"

We ran to Bus seventeen,

Barbara didn't even know why we were running.

We jumped onto Bus seventeen. I slid down in the seat and watched out the window, as Bernetta passed by on her way to Bus twenty-four,

To beat me up.

I was safe. And it was a Friday, so I was safe all weekend! But I knew that on Monday, she would beat me up. Then she didn't. I knew it would happen on Tuesday. But it didn't, not on Wednesday, or Thursday either.

Suddenly, we were in high school. For the first time, I found a group of friends that I felt super comfortable with. I rarely saw Bernetta; we were in different circles. She was in sports, and I was in drama, and our paths rarely crossed.

On Monday of my last week in high school, I had an assignment due in sixth-period History. I was leaving early that day, so during first period, I got a pass to turn in the assignment. I walked into the history classroom, put my assignment on the teacher's desk, and turned to leave the room.

As I walked between the rows of desks, looking at the floor, the other shoe finally dropped. Literally. A big sneaker blocked my way. I looked from the shoe up into the face of Donna Downs, the biggest, meanest jockette at my high school. She squinted, looking me up one side and down the other.

I braced myself.

"Hey. In middle school, did you really beat up Bernetta Thrasher?"

All it takes is a little seed of truth.

Darci Tucker tells folktales and fairytales, portrays women from American history, and trains educators to teach through storytelling. In 2000, after working at Colonial Williamsburg for thirteen years, Darci founded American Lives: History Brought to Life. She specializes in first-person portrayals of ordinary Americans who lived during extraordinary times, and has portrayed more than fifteen women from American history in schools, libraries, and other educational settings.

The Empty Pot

A CHINESE FOLKTALE
KEREN DIANE LEE

ONCE UPON A TIME, LONG AGO IN CHINA, there was a young boy named Ping. And Ping had quite the green thumb. Any plant he touched would just burst into bloom. Whether it was flowers, herbs, vegetables, you name it. It would grow like magic. And guess what? The kingdom that Ping lived in loved flowers. When you opened the door, you would set your eyes on rows and rows of flowers as far as the eye could see. And the air smelled like sweet botanical perfume.

Guess who also loved flowers? The Emperor of the land. The Emperor had his very own garden that he tended every single day. Only he was allowed in. And that sounds like a pretty perfect life: flowers, flowers, and more flowers. What more could a person ask for, right? But there was only one tiny issue. The Emperor was getting older. He didn't have anyone to take his place, and he needed to find someone. But the question was, *who?* Or *how?* He didn't have any young children or any sons, and there wasn't some special emperor selection process already in place at the palace. So, he thought, and he thought, and then he went out to his garden and thought some more until ... He came up with an idea. Ahha, I know who should pick the next emperor— the thing I love most in this world: my flowers.

Yes, you all heard right! He wanted his flowers to pick the next emperor. Yes I know. We all would've chosen something a little different. But his flowers were going to choose. So, he strolled into his grand office and sat down with flowers on his mind, and he started writing out the document to send to the villagers. This document said: "On this date, all the children of the land shall come to the palace. This will begin the process of picking the next emperor. Attendance is mandatory. Love, Emperor." When all the people in the land received the document, they were excited, elated even, because could you imagine an opportunity to be a king or an emperor? All the kids were excited, and all their parents were excited. They just couldn't wait.

On the set date, everyone headed down to the palace, Ping included. The people crowded inside the building and sat down to await further instructions. When everything was settled, the Emperor came out and began to address the audience: "Today, I shall begin the emperor selection process. But in order for me to choose, you will have to complete a challenge. It will be a challenge that the flowers

195

will be involved in, of course. I will give you each a seed, and whoever can show me their best within a year's time will get to become the next emperor. And then he went to each person and handed each of them a seed, placing it in their palm. The Emperor made sure everyone had one seed. And with that, he sent them all home. They'd come back in a year with their best, just like he said.

Everybody headed home pretty excited, as excited as you could be about a seed. But Ping was especially excited. This was his thing. This was his sport, his talent, his life's work. Seeds, man, he loved seeds. So, when he arrived home, he went straight to work.

He brought out one of his best pots. He arranged for his best soil, placing it in the pot carefully. He smoothed it down thoroughly, sprinkled it with water, gave it just the right amount of sun, and stepped back to have a seat. He waited for the seed to grow. Yes, he stayed there all night and day. And he watched it, and watched it. After about three days had passed, nothing had sprouted.

I'm Ping. I have the green thumb. I can make this grow. Let's sit and wait a little while. Let's just wait! Maybe one week. I'll come back. So, this time he actually went to bed, and he slept. And he woke up, and he checked on the flower. And after a week, still nothing had grown. *Well,* Ping thought, *maybe I just need to change it up a bit. Maybe I need to switch his soil, switch the pot.* So, he brought an even nicer pot, and even nicer soil. And he placed the seed in carefully, smoothed the seed over with the soil, sprinkled the water over it, and moved it into the best sun. Then,

196

he went on with his work and waited for the seed to grow.

He came back after about a month, and still, nothing had worked. And he came back after about two months. Still, nothing had happened! So, he moved it one more time, where it would bask in even more sun. He waited three months, which turned into four. Four turned into six.

Soon, twelve months had passed—an entire year. And it was time for everybody to come back with their results. Well, Ping looked at his flowerpot, this empty flowerpot. He looked at everybody else's pot. A parade of people was carrying their pots down to the palace after the year. Ping felt so ashamed and so sad. He had nothing. The most beautiful thing Ping had was nothing more than the intricate designs on his pot. He looked at all the other children with their tall flowers, their beautiful spreads, and their bright colors. He had nothing.

As he was walking to the palace, he passed by one of his friends. His friend stopped him. He said, "Ping, are you really going to the emperor with an empty pot? Why can't you grow a beautiful flower like mine or the other kids? I thought that this is what you did best."

"Well, yes, I do spend most of my time making things grow, but for some reason, I just ... I just couldn't get this flower to grow. I tried everything. I've grown lots of flowers better, or at least just as good. For some reason, this flower just won't grow."

Ping's father overheard all of this. He saw how sad Ping was. Ping's father said, "What matters most is that you did your best, and you're coming to the emperor with your best and nothing more." With that, all the children headed inside. Ping joined them with his empty pot. Ping looked to his left and right when they were inside and seated. He looked in front of him and behind him. He saw all these amazing flowers. Ping saw flowers that reached the ceiling, ones that were so wide and so colorful, with every color of the rainbow. Ping felt so embarrassed. The Emperor began to walk around judging the flowers, those he had loved for many years and those he had learned to love only recently. Without fail, his face stayed straight.

The Emperor studied all of them, no matter how beautiful they were. Some observers said that, if anything, the Emperor looked almost upset. Until he came upon Ping's flower, or what wasn't a flower at all. Ping couldn't take it anymore as the Emperor looked long and hard at his barren pot. He held his face and started to cry.

Oh man, the emperor's laughing at me, It's so sad. I'm so sorry. I tried everything. The flower—or the seed—it just didn't like me. We didn't have that connection, or whatever it was I needed to get it to grow. I tried. I tried the water; I tried the soil. I tried therapy. I tried it all! I'm so sorry!

With that, the emperor's smile grew even bigger. Then he said, "Ping, I admire you. To everybody else, I do not know where you got your seeds from. The ones I gave out were boiled, so they were impossible to grow. But I admire you for coming to me with nothing but the truth and your best. So, I will award you with becoming this land's new emperor." And with that, the people of Ping's land lived happily ever after, with more flowers than ever. And they were ruled by the best and most truthful emperor ever.

So, remember, your results may not always be beautiful in the eyes of others, but they are your best, and you are on your own journey.

**Keren Diane Lee** is a high school freshman in Dallas, TX. She started telling stories in second grade and enjoys telling to young children and seniors. Social studies is her favorite subject and she's a proud member of the Caballeros Drill Team. Keren is a 2022-2023 National Youth Storyteller. Photo by Bponita Lee.

El Pollo Gallero

LARRY THOMPSON

You see me limping, and you ask why
    And I might tell you the tale
But you wouldn't believe how a forty-ounce bird
    Could put a man through hell.

It happened last summer in San Angelo
    The sun was hangin' hot and low.
To the rodeo grounds we was headed
    To see the summer's best show.

The rumor was that the centerpiece
    Of the festival in town
Was a fantastic competition
    Pitting sinew against down.

Team roping pairs from across the west
    Had gathered near 'bout noon.
To set their gear and get their draws
    And with other teams commune.

The game was roping, but the opponent here
    Was not your average calf.
No, the villain in this here ring
    Would make the audience laugh.

Big old roosters with names like Devil
    or Jalapeño Joe
Would be the roping targets
    In this Chicken Team Roping Rodeo.

Now, just like cattle, the fiercest birds
    Were given names of fame
Like Cholula Chuy and Firebrand
    or even Red-Hot Flame.

But the meanest of all was a Rhode Island Red
    That went by the name of Boudin.
The rumor was that this devil bird
    Would nibble on rocks and sand.

Boudin, they said, was mean as a coyote.
    This rooster could never be tied.
His spurs were sharp, and his fearsome stare
    Would make even wolves run and hide.

Any team that drew Boudin
    Would surely fail to win
The Chicken Team Roping title
    And its belt buckles of tin.

But this year, they said the Red would fall.
    The bird would meet his match.
For a team roping pair from the south came up
    The title they planned to catch.

The team from the south was known through the west
    With a header of legend bold
El Pollo Gallero the famous vaquero
    and his heeler, Pancho Joe.

We were all excited and ready to see
    This cowboy of western renown
For El Pollo Gallero the famous vaquero
    We knew would not let us down.

But some trouble had sprung up with Pancho Joe.
    'Seems the sheriff had put him in jail.
Missing his child support payments again
    And no money to float his bail.
Seems El Pollo Gallero, the famous vaquero,
    Would not be roping this day.
Without Pancho Joe, how could he go?
    His team was one teammate away.

We pushed back our hats and shook our heads.
    How would this cowboy compete?
'Seemed like old Boudin would once again
    Scratch his way clear of defeat.

But then, to our amaze and surprise
    El Pollo Gallero called out,
"Is there a cowboy here whose arms are strong,
    And whose heart is not filled with doubt?"

For as we had hoped, this famous roper
    Had drawn Buodin for the contest.
But he needed a heeler, a steady hand
    Without any fear in his chest.

He scanned the crowd and settled on me.
    I'm not sure why I drew his gaze,
But he motioned to me and gave me a nod
    And soon, I was on my way.

We stood in the pit, and I handled our ropes,
    And my body was covered with sweat,
But El Pollo Gallero, that famous vaquero,
    Why, his brow was not even wet.

We knew the rules and had seen the others
    Make common mistakes that day—
Like letting the chicken touch your leg
    Or knocking your partner out the way

But El Pollo Gallero, that famous vaquero,
    Just stared toward the gate
Waiting for Boudin to make his entrance
    And step into his fate.

My palms were sweaty, for I knew the tales
    Of that rooster named Boudin
And cowboys he'd injured along the way—
    Made *them* eat dirt and sand.

But El Pollo Gallero, that famous vaquero,
    Was calm as the bird took his place.
The gate was opened, and crowd fell hushed,
    And he looked me square in the face.

Hombre, he said, just stay by my side.
    That chicken has fear in his eyes!
But I didn't see it; I just saw a spark.
    And then Boudin charged with surprise!

El Pollo Gallero, that famous vaquero,
    Leapt into the air.
"No touch, no foul!" the judges called out.
    El Pollo Gallero landed with care.

Boudin turned and made for me.
    I dove to the side with a shout.
El Pollo Gallero saw his chance
    And rolled his lasso out.

But I landed on the cap of my knee.
    And my face wound up in the sand.
There I was on all fours,
    With Boudin was eyeing my can!

He headed for me, and I knew I was toast.
    His spurs would find their mark,
And I'd be sore for a month or more—
    With bruises purple and dark.

The crowd stood up and laughed and jeered.
    They knew what was comin' my way,
But El Pollo Gallero, that famous vaquero,
    Let loose with the throw of the day!

It seemed to me that time slowed down
    As I saw that rope leave his wrist.
The noose hit its mark on the neck of that bird
    And I saw Boudin start to twist.

What happened next is a mystery to me.
    But somehow, I managed a throw
As Boudin spun and tried to break free,
    I caught him and couldn't let go!

The judges ran in and called it a match.
    And I held fast to my snare.
And El Pollo Gallero, that famous vaquero,
    Stared down at Boudin with a glare.

"Well done, Amigo," he said to me,
    And I let loose of my rope.
I held my knee and cleared my throat—
    Not wanting to sound like a dope.

"No sweat," I said, "it's what I do."
    He looked at me, then turned
And El Pollo Gallero, that famous vaquero,
    Reached down and picked up the bird.

I watched him as he walked away
    With Boudin tucked under his arm
He gave the crowd a hearty wave,
    And took his cheers with charm.

Staggering to my feet I stood
    And called out after the man,
"Via Con Dios, El Pollo Gallero!
    I am your number one fan."

He turned to me and raised that bird high
    As the cheers rained down from the crowd.
"Via KFC!" he called to me.
    And I knew where that chicken was bound.

Chicken Team Roping is not for the meek.
    It can be a pain in the rear,
But if El Pollo Gallero looks your way
    Cleanse your heart of all fear!

And if the chicken you draw in the contest
    Is the descendant of Boudin—
Then dry your palms and stand your ground.
    And throw—as best you can!

Larry Thompson is an author, storyteller, and cowboy poet from Seguin, Texas. He's a professional fabulist, equally comfortable spinning tales for children and adults. Larry was honored to perform at the first Dobie Dichos gathering in Oakville, Texas, and was a Featured Teller for the George West Storyfest and the Texas Storytelling Festival. His latest audio recording, *Cowboy Spirit,* received a 2020 Will Rogers Medallion Award. Additionally, Larry is a co-host on KPFT Houston's *"So, What's Your Story?"*

207

A Tongue Is A Very Important Thing

Elizabeth Ellis

My friend Baba Ayubu Kamau was a fine storyteller. Once he told me a story from Africa I will never forget.

Obatala was a great king. Because he was a wise man, his people lived in peace, and all of them had plenty. One day as the king was looking out of his window, he saw a dead bird. A wise man knows that all things must die, even a great king.

Obatala began thinking about which of his sons should be the next king. He had many sons. He considered each of them carefully. From the oldest to the youngest, he thought about both their strengths and their weaknesses.

Which one should he choose?

When he thought about his son Orula, he stopped to

consider him more carefully. Perhaps he would be a good choice. He had an easy way with people. He was even-tempered and not quick to be angry. But a king must also be wise.

Orula was young, and his father had never taken the time to test him before.

So Obatala called Orula to him and said, "Tomorrow, I want you to go to the marketplace. Look at everything that is for sale there. Take your time, son. When you have seen everything, I want you to bring me the most wonderful thing that you can find there."

Of course, Orula was happy to go to the marketplace. It was bustling with activity. There were shoppers searching for bargains. Sellers were calling to them to come and buy.

Just as his father had asked, Orula looked carefully at everything: the gold jewelry, the carved ivory, ebony, and the beautiful cloth from foreign countries.

When he had seen everything, he chose a beef tongue.

He took it home and cooked it in fine wine and spices. Now it was sweet to smell and even better to taste. He carried the dish to his father.

Obatala was perplexed. He asked, "Of all the things you could have bought, you chose a tongue?"

Orula said, "Father, a tongue is a very important thing. With a tongue, you can praise someone's good efforts so they will work harder. With a tongue, you can give someone good advice and keep them from making a bad mistake. With a tongue, you can call out a warning to someone who is in a lot of danger. With a tongue, you can

209

comfort someone who is crying and upset. A tongue is a very important thing."

So Obatala knew that meant Orula's choice was wise, but he thought he should test him again to be sure. He said, "Tomorrow, please return to the marketplace. Look at everything that is offered for sale there. At the end of the day, bring me the worst thing you can find."

Orula did as his father asked and returned to the marketplace. Once more, he looked at everything. It did not take him long to realize that many things offered for sale were overpriced. When he looked more closely, he could see that some of them were not well made and would fall apart soon after they were purchased. Some of the things that were offered for sale were just plain silly.

When he has seen everything once more, he chose a beef tongue. He took it home and cooked it in the same loving way with the fine wine and the spices. Once more, he brought it to his father.

This time Obatala truly was astonished. He said, "Yesterday, you brought me this and said it was the most wonderful thing that you could find. Today you bring it back and say it is the worst. How is that possible?"

Orula replied, "A tongue is a very important thing. With a tongue, you can tell a lie about someone and steal their good name. With a tongue, you can trick someone out of all their money. With a tongue, you can start a quarrel between two friends. With a tongue, it is even possible to start a war between two countries. A tongue is a very important thing!"

Obatala knew that Orula was wise far beyond his years. So he made all the arrangements to make sure that Orula would be the next king.

I could hear the truth in Ayubu's story. It made me think of something that happened to me when I was in elementary school many years ago. My mind went tumbling back to a time when I was ten.

When I was a girl, I rode the school bus home in the afternoon. I don't remember how it happened, but one day I was the first person to get on the bus. That was great because that meant I'd get my pick of all the seats.

While I was sitting on the bus, I noticed my friend Nicky out on the playground. She called to me. I couldn't really understand what she was saying, so I turned sideways in the seat and pulled the window down so that I could hear her. I hoped she was asking me to go somewhere with her.

She was. She said, "My family is going to the movies on Saturday afternoon. Would you like to come with us?"

Of course, I wanted to go. I told her I would ask my mother. I hoped she would say yes.

I was so busy yelling out the window to Nicky about going to the movies, I didn't even notice my feet. They were sticking out into the aisle.

The next person who got on the bus was an eighth-grade girl. She was a lot bigger than I was. She was a lot meaner than I was, too. When she came down the aisle of the bus, she tripped over my feet.

Well, she didn't really fall all the way to the floor of the bus. With her hands, she managed to catch herself on the seatbacks. I couldn't understand why she was so angry.

But she was. No matter how many times I apologized, she wouldn't stop hitting me. Every time I said I was sorry, she just pounded on me again.

She struck me so that my eye began to swell up. Pretty soon, I couldn't see out of it at all. When I got home and looked in the bathroom mirror, I could see that I had what people call a "black eye."

After four or five days, it wasn't a "black eye" anymore. It had turned purple.

Four or five days after that, it wasn't purple anymore. It had turned green.

And then it turned that disgusting shade of yellow that bruises turn right before they heal up altogether.

That was almost seventy years ago. My eye hasn't hurt in many, many years.

But the thing that girl said to me just before she hit me, that part still hurts.

Orula was right. A tongue is a very important thing.

 **Elizabeth Ellis** is the recipient of both the National Storytelling Network's Lifetime Achievement and Circle of Excellence Awards. She uses her awards to press wildflowers. She is the author of *From Plot to Narrative, Prepare to Scare* and *Every Day a Holiday* (Parkhurst Brothers Publishers) and co-author with Loren Niemi of *Inviting the Wolf In: Thinking About Difficult Stories.* She lives in Dallas. Photo by Kate Dudding.

Wylie Mae and the Hairy Man
JIAAN POWERS

WYLIE MAE LIVED WITH HER MOMMA AND HER DADDY north of Beaumont and south of Kountze. They lived in the country out near the woods that led into the forest and swamps of the Neches River there in Texas. Now, Wylie Mae didn't have much, but she had her dogs. She loved those dogs. She could be found outside throwing sticks and playing around with her dogs, no matter the cold or the heat.

One day, her momma called to her from the front porch, "Wylie Mae! Come get this bag and go get some kindling."

"Yes, Momma." Wylie Mae grabbed the kindling bag. "Come on, dogs," she called as she scampered down the steps.

"Wylie Mae, go and tie up those dogs."

"Momma, not my dogs."

"Wylie Mae."

"Pleeease."

"WYLIE MAE!"

"Yes, mam."

"Before you go, come back in here, Wylie Mae. Look there on the table. Just in case, I've put a spell on that glass of milk. If anything happens to you, that milk will turn red as rubies, and I'll let your dogs loose to come find you."

"Okay, Momma."

Wylie Mae tied up her dogs and went way across the yard to the big old oak tree near the edge of the woods. It was warm and sunny. Days in Texas could be like that, even in the middle of January.

Wylie Mae started picking up sticks, putting them in her bag. There had been a windy storm recently, and branches were everywhere. She had the bag full in no time. As she turned to head back to the house, she heard a whole mess of birds flying and twittering. She could even hear their poop landing on the leaves on the ground.

"I bet those are Cedar Waxwings," Wylie Mae said right out loud. She headed into the woods. Up ahead through the bare trees, she spotted maybe fifty or a hundred little brown and gray, lemon-yellow birds. She heard their high, thin whistles. "Yep, Cedar Waxwings." Wylie Mae hurried on. Now she could see their dark masks and topknots, the red spots on their wings, and yellow tips on their tails. She watched the birds cover the Possum Haws. When they had eaten all the red-orange berries on those little trees, they

215

swooped away deeper toward the forest and the swamps. Wylie Mae was mesmerized. She knew they would strip all the berries off the Possum Haws all the way to the river. Wylie Mae followed. She loved Cedar Waxwings.

"AH-CHOO!"

Wylie Mae turned around really slow. There stood an old man wearing old pants, old shoes, and an old shirt. He was dirty and had hair all over his face, long old eyebrows tucked behind his hairy old ears. He was wiping his nose on his hairy old hand.

"Good morning, Mr. Hairy Man! That's sure a bad cold you have!"

"How do you know my name?"

Wylie Mae knew. The hairy man had chased her momma's brother, Wylie, all out in the swamps near the river. Her Uncle Wylie had always gotten away.

"Just do, sir."

"How'd you know I have a cold?" He sneezed again, "AH-CHOO!"

The hairy man wiped his nose again on his hairy old hand.

"What's your name, girl?"

"Wylie Mae, sir."

"Wylie Mae, I'm hungry, and I'm gonna eat you!"

Wylie Mae threw her bag at the hairy man and took off running. She was fast.

Back at the house, that glass of milk had turned red as rubies. Wylie Mae's momma rushed to untie the dogs. They took off running and barking and racing to find Wylie Mae.

They were fast.

"*Rooooof, Roooof, Roooof!*"

The hairy man stopped in his tracks. "Wylie Mae, what's that I hear?"

"Them's my dogs, Mr. Hairy Man."

"I don't like dogs!"

Then Wylie Mae's dogs were barking and howling and chasing the hairy man off toward the river.

Wylie Mae went back and gathered up her bag of kindling. She got home safe and sound. Later, her dogs got home, too, safe and sound.

Time went by, and spring came. Wylie Mae's daddy was home from working on the rigs out in the Gulf. They loved going fishing together. They took the road to the fishing place on the river. It wasn't far. They walked. Wylie Mae told her daddy about meeting up with the hairy man. Told him how her dogs had chased the hairy man away.

"You be careful there, Baby Girl."

"I am, Daddy."

They fished and fished. Got some Bass. Then they ate their egg salad sandwiches and drank their Coca-Colas. Talked and laughed. Fished some more.

Wylie Mae was standing close to the slippery edge of the bank of the river when her daddy hollered, "Wylie Mae, look out!" He grabbed her back toward him.

She screamed. "Daddy, is it the hairy man?"

"Look there." Her daddy pointed to the river.

Wylie Mae wasn't afraid of snakes, but there was the biggest water moccasin she had ever seen, not ten inches away from the slippery edge. That was enough excitement for Wylie Mae and her daddy. They packed up and headed home.

Wylie Mae's momma fried up those Bass in cooking oil. And she fried up hush puppies, little corn muffins mixed with chopped bits of onion. Over dinner Wylie Mae and her momma and her daddy laughed at Wylie Mae for thinking the hairy man had been at the river.

Yet that night, Wylie Mae prayed, "Thank you, God, for just an old poisonous snake and NOT Mr. Hairy Man."

Come summertime, Wylie Mae's daddy was back at work. She was out in the yard playing with her dogs when her momma hollered from the porch.

"Wylie Mae, come get this bucket. Those blackberries at the edge of the woods ought to be ripe for picking. You get enough, and I'll bake us a cobbler for lunch."

Wylie Mae loved her momma's cobbler. The pastry all rolled out and laid in the smaller of the two iron skillets. Plenty of sugar and butter and just enough cinnamon and a bit of flour, all mixed up with the berries and then baked crispy brown on top. Oh, just the thought made Wylie Mae's mouth water.

"Come on, dogs!"

"Wylie Mae, you go tie them dogs up. I want you back here before noon, so I can get the cobbler in the oven. Just in case, there's a glass of milk on the table. I put a spell on it. Anything happens, it will turn red as rubies, and I'll let your dogs loose."

Wylie Mae didn't even complain. She was thinking

about cobbler. She stopped long enough to pick some mint growing in the garden. She rubbed it all over her to keep the mosquitoes off. She set out past the old oak tree to the edge of the woods to the blackberry bushes. Bees were everywhere, butterflies and insects, too. Wylie Mae knew to stay calm so the bees wouldn't sting her. As she picked the berries, she took time to pop some in her mouth. Yum. She didn't mind the juicy berries turning her fingers purple. Wylie Mae had just filled her bucket to the top when this big butterfly came fluttering by her head.

She held her bucket ever so careful.

"Whoa, look at you. Miss Tiger Swallowtail," Wylie Mae said right out loud. "You must be five inches across." She knew it was female by the blue along the bottom of its yellow and black wings, plus it had tiny orange spots. The butterfly floated beyond the berry bushes to the honeysuckle. Then, it headed off toward the forest, swamps, and the river. Wylie Mae followed. She loved Tiger Swallowtails.

"AH-CHOO!"

No, it couldn't be, thought Wylie Mae. She hadn't gone that far. Had she? Wylie Mae turned around. Real slow.

"Mr. Hairy Man, you still got that cold?"

"How did you know?"

The hairy man wiped his nose on his hairy old hand.

"Just do, sir."

"Well, I'm real hungry, and I'm gonna eat you!"

Wylie Mae threw her bucket at him and took off running fast. The hairy man didn't even stop to eat any berries. He was after Wylie Mae. She kept running. He did, too.

Where were her dogs?

Back home, Wylie Mae's momma had taken the rag rug out to the porch railing and was beating it with her broom to get it clean. She didn't see the glass of milk on the table turn red as rubies.

Meanwhile, Wylie Mae could hear the hairy man getting closer, sneezing, and wheezing.

"AH-CHOO!"

Suddenly, Wylie Mae saw a good climbing tree, and she shimmied right to the top.

"Girl, come on down out of that tree."

Without her dogs, Wylie Mae had to think fast. She remembered her Uncle Wylie.

"Mr. Hairy Man, I heard you could conjure some spells."

"I can."

"I bet you can't make rope appear everywhere."

"Yes, I can."

"Prove it!"

"Easy. ROPE! Appear everywhere."

And just like that, rope was everywhere. Hanging from the trees. Coiled on the ground. Everywhere.

"Now I'm getting away from you, Mr. Hairy Man! I can grab this rope and just swing on out of here. To catch me, you'd have to make all the rope disappear everywhere."

The hairy man scratched his hairy old head. "ROPE, DISAPPEAR EVERYWHERE!"

The rope was gone. Gone from the trees and the ground. Gone. Even the rope tying up Wylie Mae's dogs disappeared. Her dogs took off running and barking and racing fast across the yard, past the old oak tree, past the berry bushes into the woods, tearing to the river to find her.

"*Rooooof, Roooof, Roooof!*"

"Girl, what's that I hear?"

"Them's my dogs, Mr. Hairy Man."

"I don't like dogs."

And then there they were, Wylie Mae's dogs, barking and howling and chasing the hairy man off toward the river.

Wylie Mae climbed down out of the tree, picked up all the berries, and got on home safe and sound. She worried about her dogs.

Her momma had just taken that sweet-smelling, crispy-brown cobbler out of the oven when Wylie Mae's dogs showed up scratching at the screen door. She went out and hugged and hugged her dogs. Their paws were covered with dirt and some sand. Wylie Mae never did see the hairy man again. She and her momma figured maybe her dogs had chased him deep into the forest and swamps right out into some quicksand pit, and that was the end of him.

Ever after, Wylie Mae's momma always let her take her dogs with her, just in case.

Jiaan Powers grew up in Beaumont and currently lives in Dallas with her husband and numerous cats. She has been a professional storyteller for a long time, even longer than the twenty-two years she taught public school. Once, a mouse ran up Jiaan's pants leg, but that's another story. She would love to hear your story. Learn more at jiaanpowers@jiaanpowers.com. Photo by Gary Patton.

The Spaghetti Tree

Connie Neil Fisher

THE FAMILY WAS NESTLED IN AFTER SUPPER. There were our three children: Neil, age seven, Stuart, five, and Leta, three, plus my wife Dolores and myself. Those ages are approximate because I cannot remember just what year it was. I think it was 1965.

We were watching the Education Channel out of Oklahoma City when a production from the BBC (British Broadcasting System), presented a documentary narrated by the then Prime Minister of England, Ian Wilson. It was about the Italian spaghetti harvest of 1962. I told the kids to pay attention because their daddy had been at the first full spaghetti harvest after WWII in the fall of 1947.

Nineteen forty-seven was a good year to be starting in the U.S. Army. WWII was history, and no one expected to be shot. Europe was cleaning up, and Italy was a little ahead of France and Germany. No one knew about the Russian situation. As I was saying, 1947 was a good year. Most GIs were leaving the services, but the jobs were still there, so it was an excellent opportunity for fast promotion.

As a late-August graduate of MFSS (Medical Field Service School) of San Antonio, Texas, I did not expect to have to bandage any combat wounds. I expected a "take two aspirin and call me tomorrow" type of existence.

Our troop ship, called the *Nonesuch*, docked at the little port of Canard in Italy. For two days, the troops were kept on the boat before we disembarked and went directly to busses or duce-and-a-halfs (2.5-ton troop transport trucks). There were about four hundred of us medics, infantry, signal, ordnance, quartermaster, and truck drivers—a real mixed bag of replacements.

Each truck was packed with a mix of MOSs (Military Occupation Specialists) departing for their future assignments. It didn't take long for the GIs to be processed and sent on their way. After all names but one were called and moved, one lonesome dog face sat on his duffel bag, waiting. "Fisher!" said the Sergeant, "Stay put. There will be transportation for you soon." Then the Sergeant took off in a jeep.

I was left there, alone. I'm from Sand Springs, Oklahoma, and I know little towns, but this town, hamlet, or whatever, wasn't as big as Bug Tussle. The transport we had been on was a commercial ship so there were no American sailors around, no other GIs. The civilians went about their business.

At mid-afternoon, a jeep with a trailer and driver pulled up. The driver, a corporal, said, "Are you Fisher?"

"Yes," I said.

"Damn," he said. "Hop in!"

My gear was pitched into the back of the jeep. We went about a hundred yards without a word spoken when we came to a small compound. The Corporal jumped out and handed some papers to a couple of Italian police guards. Some laborers close at hand loaded the trailer, and we took off.

"My name is Chance," said the driver. I introduced myself. "You're one hell of a disappointment," said Chance. "We were expecting a female. What the hell are you doing with a name like Connie? The Captain picked you special because of your name. We thought to smell some perfume."

"I have some Old Spice," I said. We rode on in silence.

The road led through some very beautiful hills, and as we topped one, the view before us was a long, wide valley filled with spaghetti trees. Each tree was so covered it looked like a field of snow broken by rows for harvesters. "We are in luck," said Chance. "It's the first full harvest since the war." He meant WWII. "There will be a big spaghetti festival soon."

My billet was in a former Italian military facility. Our unit consisted of a medical doctor, a captain, myself, a Pfc. medic, Chance, the driver, and an administrative sergeant. We four were part of a Civil Affairs unit that worked closely with the local health people. I was there to help the doctor and, when needed, to assist any MASH unit within a ten-mile radius.

One of the most intriguing places for me was an old prisoner of war camp with off-limits signs all over the place, guarded by Italian police or military. A lot went on in there, but it was hush-hush.

~~~

I had time after normal work hours to visit around and to watch the harvest. Growing up in Oklahoma, I had never thought about how spaghetti came to the stores. It came from far-off places like Minnesota.

The laden trees were harvested by workers with a spool, who would attach one end and then roll it up. The laborers worked from wagons or truck beds. To be elevated helped. Occasionally a strand would break, and the doffer would use soft pasta to join the ends. I always hated it when I tasted a pasta patch, then continued to roll. Truckloads of spools would go to the processing plant. There, they were unspooled by teenage girls where the spaghetti went through a cleansing solution to remove dirt and bugs and was then placed in drying and stretching racks, after which it was packaged. During the festival, it went directly from cleaning to hot water and then to the bowls.

That secret facility really bothered me, but the Italians were so used to secrets that they just accepted it, or seemed to. If my captain knew anything, he didn't talk to me. Chance was always on the go, and the sergeant was up to his ears in paperwork. I just did my work; the civilian medical people mostly wanted me to bring supplies.

I had been there about three weeks when I was called to the hush-hush facility. There had been a scaffold break, and people were hurt. I grabbed a couple of traction splints, my medical pack, got Chance, and took off. They would not let Chance in. I entered the compound and was taken to a building. I entered, and then beheld a big greenhouse with rows of bonsai-type trees laden with the first-ever "Angel Hair Spaghetti"—really thin spaghetti. I was taken to where several men were reclining against a wall. Some scaffolding had broken, and the men had fallen. The local doctor was there. He assigned me some patch-up, Iodine type work, but he took my traction splints. We were there for about two hours and sworn to secrecy. I then departed.

The long and the short of the story is that two weeks later, the whole community was invited to witness the first-ever Angel Hair Spaghetti harvest. It was really different. They had made it thin and fortified it with iron and discovered that the iron had gone to the very tip of the strand. That gave them the idea to use magnets to harvest.

That is why they had the scaffolding. Overhead they had placed showerhead-like openings with magnets inside each opening. They would lower the magnets over the tree, and the Angel Hair spaghetti would rise like a Cobra snake, then ascend into the tube where it was washed, formed, dried, cut, and packaged in one continuous process.

Almost all of the first Angel Hair spaghetti was consumed at the first festival that followed. Some of the older citizens refused to eat that new stuff. You could just see them thinking, *It had to be bad for you.*

Not long after that momentous event, I was transferred to Fitzsimmons General Hospital, Aurora, Colorado, U.S. of A.

"Yep," I told the family, "I was there. Now it's just like it was, except that now they use portable magnet doffers, and that spaghetti queen looks like the daughter of the one I saw."

Now, some of you may think that I am just making this up, that I was never there. But I'll give you a task. Get some angel hair spaghetti and a magnet, and see if one end comes up. If not, then it's not true Canard Angel Hair Spaghetti.

 The late **Connie Neil Fisher** was born in Guthrie, Oklahoma, and grew up in Sand Springs. He retired from the Army Reserves as a Lt. Colonel and later retired from the public school system after more than thirty years as a vocal music teacher. As a professional storyteller, he captivated audiences of all ages with a unique voice and an extensive repertoire of tales. He was a member of The Tejas Storytelling Association, The National Storytelling Network, Tulsy Town Yarnspinners, Tallgrass Tellers, and Territory Tellers. Photo by Chester Weems

Under the Influence of the Silver Screen

MARY ANN BLUE

IT WAS 1953, AND I WAS ALMOST FIVE YEARS OLD. It seemed like everyone in Pittsburgh County, Oklahoma, was singing the Patti Page hit "How Much is that Doggie in the Window?" and dancing and humming to the tunes of Bob Wills and His Texas Playboys, who played every now and then at the Naval Ammunition Depot in McAlester. My family lived two blocks away, and we could hear them on Saturday nights when they were in town. We would sit on our front porch, listening to their Western swing music and waiting for Bob's iconic intro to Leon McAuliffe's guitar solo, "Take it away, Leon!".

One day, my father came home with a big announcement. We were moving to Tulsa. I asked him if we could still hear Bob Wills on our new front porch. His answer was no. When we sat on our porch in McAlester, Bob Wills was playing just for me. We couldn't move! I was going to marry Bob Wills! But move we did. My father had bought the Admiral Drive-in Theatre, soon to become the number one entertainment spot in Tulsa, and life for the Blues would never be the same.

I was lonely at first. I had my dog, Mutt, and my big brother, Phil, but there weren't any families yet in our brand-new neighborhood. Phil was six years older than I was and didn't have much time for me in those days. But I had a rather impressive group of imaginary friends who had recently built an apartment on the non-existent second floor of our house. The newly crowned Queen Elizabeth came to have tea regularly with my dolls and me, and she sometimes brought her boy, Charles. He was just my age!

The drive-in was a family business, and we were all involved in one way or another. My dad worked day and night to get it off the ground. My mother filled in at the box office when someone called in sick, and she designed all the newspaper ads for the drive-in that ran in the *Tulsa World* and the *Tulsa Tribune*. I like to say that our family lived under the influence of the silver screen.

One of the first pictures my dad showed at the drive-in was *Gentlemen Prefer Blondes* with Jane Russell and Marilyn Monroe. I immediately assumed the identity of Loralei Lee, Marilyn's character. I walked around the house in my bathing suit and pair of my mother's high heels, talking in a high-pitched Marilyn voice, and answered only to the names Loralei or Marilyn for weeks and weeks.

As the years went by, I spent lots of time at the Admiral Drive-in, and my imaginary world really came alive there. Daddy and I had a Saturday afternoon routine. After breakfast, we would head out for the drive-in. Daddy would spend a few hours "working on the books," as he called it, and I was his secretary. My main job was playing on the adding machine, but he also let me answer the phone and give out showtimes. We practiced together so that I could say everything correctly, and I loved doing it. As I got older, my dad let me stamp his signature onto pads of free passes. He liked to give out lots of passes.

When I got tired of office work, I'd head into the concession stand, fix myself a "suicide" out of every flavor of soda, and the concession stand would become my own private movie set. *Tammy and the Bachelor* was playing at the drive-in, and I was Debbie Reynolds. As Tammy, I would sing and dance around that huge empty space. I'd pause to look thoughtfully into space and sing, "I hear the Cottonwoods whispering above, Tammy, Tammy, Tammy's in love."[3] Sometimes I was Doris Day, singing softly about that dreamy Rock Hudson, then getting mad at him and stomping off. If I got lucky, it would start to rain, and I'd head outside so that I could be

---

3. "Tammy," from the film *Tammy and the Bachelor (1957)*. Writer/s: Jay Livingston, Raymond B. Evans, Publisher: Kanjian Music, Warner Chappell Music, Inc., Wixen Music Publishing.

Gene Kelly, just dancin' and singin' in the rain![4] I starred in lots of movies at that concession stand. I was Shirley Jones in *Oklahoma!* Rose-mary Clooney in *White Christmas,* and Mitzi Gaynor in *South Pacific!*

I didn't usually play on the playground. After all, I had the entire drive-in as my playground. So, I saddled up my imaginary horse, Lightnin', and rode the range, just lookin' for trouble. The drive-in was full of danger if you were on horseback, flooded rivers raging out of their banks, rattlesnakes that could spook your horse and bite and kill you before you could say Jack Robinson, and roaming bands of outlaws, all after your hide. I explored every inch of the drive-in on Saturday afternoons, except for one place. It wasn't exactly forbidden to go there; it was simply unthinkable. I shouldn't go there; I mustn't go there. But it beckoned me; it lured me. Let me get this straight; I was not afraid to go there. Growing up at the drive-in, I knew real drive-in movie fear, and I'm not just talking about quicksand! Real drive-in movie fear was being eaten alive by African Army Ants. Real drive-in movie fear was taking a bullet in the gut in a robbery and having to wake up a vet in the middle of the night to take the bullet out ... a vet who could be trusted to keep his mouth shut! Real drive-in movie fear was being sent to the chair for a murder you didn't commit!

---

4.   "Singing in the Rain", lyrics by Arthur Freed, music by Nacio Herb Brown (1929), from the musical of the same name starring Gene Kelly and Debbie Reynolds (1957).

There was one place where my mother had absolutely forbidden me to go. When the drive-in was open to customers, I was absolutely forbidden to go anywhere near the back few ramps of the drive-in. It was forbidden, so of course, I had to check it out! I walked back there one night while my mom was working at the box office. On the screen, an advertisement for Dr. Pepper was playing, "Go man go, it's not very far, shake it on down to that cool snack bar! Come on, Jill, give us a treat! A friendly pepper-upper with a tasty beat! Drink Dr. Pepper, Doc-doctor Pepper, 'cause it never lets you down! Frosty, man, frosty!" When I got there, I couldn't understand why it was off-limits. There was nothing to see, just row after row of empty cars.

On this particular Saturday afternoon, I was starring in *Gunfight at the OK Corral,* and I was not going to be Rhonda Fleming. No, today I was taking over for Kirk Douglas as Doc Holliday, and I did not always follow the regular script. Today, I was wounded in a gunfight, but it was a flesh wound. They gave me a swig of whisky straight from the bottle and patched me up. I stumbled back onto the street; it was Tombstone. I saw Marshal Wyatt Earp, played by Burt Lancaster. He was calling up to a bad guy, played by Dennis Hopper, holed up in a hotel room on the second floor. "Billy, throw down your gun and come out!"

I walked into the saloon, and the bartender handed me a shot glass of whisky and warned me, "Doc, you're walking into a stacked deck." But I was ready, ready to do the unthinkable. It was now or never. I loosened my six-gun in its holster, and I walked, big as you please, through the

233

MEN'S RESTROOM DOOR!!

I don't know what I expected, but this was a real letdown. It just looked like a regular restroom: stalls on one side, lavatories on the other. I turned to leave, and that's when I saw it! This was great, better than I had hoped for! But what on earth was it? It was white porcelain and was hanging on the wall. It was too high, too long, and too narrow to be a bathtub. It really looked more like a horse trough. But in my wildest imagination, and I had one all right, I couldn't imagine John Wayne bringing his horse in there for a drink of water. I would have to ask Phil what it was. My big brother knew everything worth knowing.

Phil worked at the drive-in as a member of what they simply called "the crew." For the most part, the crew was primarily made up of a group of boys who'd had a brush or two with the law and couldn't get a job elsewhere. Our dad lived under the influence of Spencer Tracy as Father Flanagan in *Boys' Town.* He felt sure that if Spencer Tracy could get Mickey Rooney back on track, then Alex Blue could do the same thing with these boys. He gave them a chance, some loving guidance, and he reached out a helping hand. And it worked, at least for some of them.

The Admiral Drive-in crew all lived under the influence of James Dean in *Rebel without a Cause.* They wore their hair slicked back with plenty of Brylcreem, tight blue jeans, and white t-shirts, some with a pack of cigarettes rolled into the sleeve. Some of them wore black leather jackets. My brother bought a pair of black cowboy boots with white eagles on the sides and practiced his sneer in the mirror.

234

During the day, the crew picked up trash, put the speakers back on the posts, changed the marquee, and sometimes got to scale the screen tower. At night, they worked in the concession stand. Their favorite duty was catching people who were "running the exit." To run the exit successfully, you waited until dark and eased down Archer Street, which ran along the side of the drive-in, with your headlights off. You stopped just short of the exit and watched the box office. When they got busy and were distracted, you gunned the engine, took off fast through the exit, and whipped into a parking place. If you were lucky, you were home free! If you were spotted by the box office, they pressed a button, and a buzzer went off in the concession stand. A crew member shouted, "They're running the exit!" The doors to the concession stand flew open, and half a dozen members of the crew ran out the doors, flashlights blazing. They would surround your car and demand to see your ticket stubs! My brother told me that once the crew hopped into Leon Carter's Chevy and chased a car that ran the exit all the way down Admiral Boulevard, going sixty miles an hour! There was indeed certain danger as well as irony attached to being busted by the Admiral Drive-in crew.

Another way to sneak into the drive-in was called "back ramping," climbing the fence behind the back ramp of the drive-in. Back rampers were easy to spot; they sat on the patio by the concession stand and were the only ones on the patio wearing torn jeans. Back rampers would never stand out today because of their jeans. Today their jeans would merely be a fashion statement.

The most popular method of sneaking into the drive-in, the king of unlawful entry, was hiding in the trunk of the car. If you didn't weigh much, you stood a good chance of not getting caught. If you got greedy and packed too many folks in the trunk, you were sure to get busted. It was well known that my mother was very good at noticing suspicious cars. They said that Elsie Blue could spot a low-riding car at fifty yards. One night my mother was going to work at the box office. She stopped on her way to pick up some bread at the Colonial Grocery on Admiral Boulevard. As she was leaving the store, she noticed two teenagers climbing into the big trunk of a '51 Buick. She got into her car and drove to the drive-in. A few minutes later, as soon as she opened the box office, that same Buick came through the line. She called out to Art Percy, who was taking money for tickets, "Art, that will be fifty cents apiece for the two in the front seat and fifty cents apiece for the two in the trunk." Without opening the trunk, they paid up, and my mother became a living legend among the drive-in crew.

When my brother wasn't working at the drive-in, Phil was singing baritone with an a capella quartet called The Four Barons. They sang that popular intricate harmony doo-wop music of the fifties, with poetic lyrics like "sh-boom, sh-boom, rata-ta-tata-ta-tata-ta-ta" and asked probing questions like "Why must I be a teenager in love?" They wore white sports coats with pink carnations in their lapels when they performed. Fifteen-year-old girls would follow Phil home from school and fling themselves on our front porch. Phil was in heaven.

During this time, Phil fell in love with Gloria Jones, known to her public simply as Glo. She had platinum blonde hair, slicked back in a ducktail, just like Kim Novak. She wore tight sweaters and tight skirts and lots of blue eye shadow. Phil was walking on air; he wanted the world to know that Glo was his girlfriend.

The drive-in crew had been experimenting with home-made tattoos, mostly just initials or tiny crosses. Phil had watched members of the crew practice their art but didn't participate, not until he fell in love with Glo. Then he decided to tattoo Glo onto his arm. He got a needle and some India ink, and he went to work.

It was a discreet tattoo as tattoos go, small block letters, all caps, dark blue ink, *GLO,* on his left wrist. He placed it strategically so that he could cover it with his long sleeve or his watch so that our mother wouldn't see it. These were the nineteen fifties, and no one had tattoos, no one except sailors, circus performers, and members of motorcycle gangs. Things were going great for Phil for about three days. Our mother hadn't seen it, and feedback from the ninth grade at Bell Junior High fell somewhere between cool and shocking. But then Phil checked into the Heartbreak Hotel. Gloria Jones broke up with Phil and left him with a broken heart and, you might say, a "glo-ing" arm.

Phil was a creative thinker, and he decided to change his tattoo. He was taking first year Spanish at the time, so he checked the dictionary in the back of his "El Camino Real" Spanish textbook. He found that "lobo" was the Spanish word for wolf. He figured he could live his life with Lobo on his arm. So, he added a "BO" onto the end of "GLO." Now all he had to do was get rid of the "G"! His friend, Gordy McFadden, had read in a magazine that you could get rid of a tattoo the same way you put it on, except using buttermilk instead of ink. Phil got some buttermilk and went to work again. The "G" didn't budge. Phil lived the rest of his life with a Spanish word on his arm all right—*GLOBO,* which means balloon. Not nearly the effect he was hoping for.

Phil always claimed that our mother didn't find out about the Globo tattoo until a year later, something I never believed. But her way of letting him know that she knew was brilliant. Our mother lived under the influence of every Hollywood musical she had ever seen, and she'd seen them all! She simply walked into his room one night while he was doing his algebra homework and quoted a line from a song in an Irving Berlin musical playing at the drive-in. She said, "Phil, a sailor's not a sailor 'til a sailor's been tattooed!"[5] Then she turned on her heel and walked out of his room. She never mentioned his tattoo again.

---

5.   Lyrics and music by Irving Berlin. From the musical *There's No Business Like Show Business* (1954).

In the late fifties, our dad expanded the Admiral Drive-in into a twin drive-in, and the Admiral Twin became the largest drive-in in the Southwest. When the crowds were big, I worked in the concession stand as I got older. Even though I spent fewer Saturday afternoons at the drive-in, I did learn to drive at the Admiral Twin. My dad would toss me the keys to his Pontiac and warn, "Don't hit any speaker posts!" and I'd drive up and down the ramps, looking for Troy Donahue.

I grew up on Route 66 at the Admiral Twin. I saw Elvis make his screen debut in *Love Me Tender.* Alfred Hitchcock scared the daylights out of me in *Psycho.* I witnessed more gunfights, cattle drives, and saloon brawls than any other kid around. But my favorite memories will always be the ones when I co-starred with Debbie Reynolds, Doris Day, Rock Hudson, and Kirk Douglas in the Saturday afternoon matinee at the drive-in movies.

Mary Ann Blue is rumored to have a strange Spanish word tattooed on her wrist. This story is less peculiar than you think because Mary Ann is a retired Spanish teacher and has used storytelling to teach language for over forty years. She has also enjoyed mentoring youth storytellers for many years. Mary Ann has been a Texas Storytelling Festival featured teller and has served the festival in many leadership roles. Photo by Jacob Virgin

239

The Long Haired Girl
ADAPTED FROM A CHINESE DONG MINORITY FOLKTALE
NANCY WANG, ETH-NOH-TEC

LONG AGO IN ANCIENT CHINA, there was a village in a valley surrounded by mountains. The people of the village were kind to each other and were happy, even though the creek that ran through their village had been dry for years. They had been suffering from a drought.

As a result, the people had a very hard time growing the necessary vegetables in their gardens. There was not enough water to quench their thirst, not enough to bathe more than once a month. The people were doing their best to survive with each other, but the drought was beginning to look as if there would be no end.

In order to get water, they had to walk miles to the nearest stream. Back and forth daily was their plight.

One day, a young girl of the village, the Long Haired

Girl, whose long black hair flowed to her waist, was out on a nearby mountain picking plants for their pigs and herbs for her mother, who was bedridden with a sickness. On this morning as she scavenged and picked, she came across a huge turnip!

"Why, this turnip will feed us for weeks!"

She began to tug and pull at the top greens of the turnip to remove it from the ground. When she had succeeded, to her utter surprise, a gush of water came flowing out from the hole which had held that turnip!

"Oh my!" and the Long Haired Girl bent down to taste the water.

But, before she could reach the water, that huge turnip wrangled itself out from her grip, flew up into the air, plunged down and plugged up the hole in the ground. The water stopped flowing.

"But I wanted to taste that water ... hmmm."

Once again, she began to pull at the greens. Out came the turnip; out flowed the water, and the Long Haired Girl quickly bent down, scooped up some water into the palm of her free hand and sipped.

"Sweet and fresh!"

But the moment she uttered those words, the turnip once again flew out of her hand, plugged up the hole and this time, the Long Haired girl was spun into the air and landed in front of the very large Spirit King of the Mountain.

"You have discovered the secret of my mountain. Tell no one or I shall take your life!

"But if the waters are allowed to flow to my village,

the people will not have to suffer!"

"Quiet! Tell no one or you are dead! Now be gone!"

The Long Haired Girl was spun up into the air and soon she found herself at the foot of the mountain.

Frightened, she told no one of the secret waters.

Every day, the Long Haired Girl struggled keeping the secret. Every day, she watched her neighbors old and young, trudge miles to the nearest stream for water, then return those many miles with the weight of the water in their jugs.

Soon neighbors began to notice a change in the girl:

"What is wrong with the Long Haired Girl?"

"She looks so pale."

"Her long black hair has turned all white!"

"I think she is dying!"

And she was dying—dying from the truth untold.

Suddenly, an old man stumbled, dropped his jug of water, and fell to the ground!

"Old man, *gung gung,* you've hurt yourself. Oh my! You've broken your leg. It is bleeding! It's all my fault! What a coward I've been!"

The Long Haired Girl could take it no longer!

As the crowd gathered to help the old man the Long Haired Girl cried out:

"Everyone, listen! There's a stream of fresh sweet water!" and she pointed at the mountain.

"I have seen it with my own eyes! Come I will take you there! Bring your shovels for the water is beneath a very large turnip and the turnip must be destroyed before it plugs up the hole in the ground from where the water flows!"

When the villagers got there, indeed they pulled up the turnip, chopped it into pieces, and out flowed the sweet water all the way down to their village.

As the villagers cheered, danced and celebrated, suddenly, the Long Haired Girl was nowhere to be found.

"The Long Haired Girl must have already gone down to tell her mother the good news."

But this was not so.

High up on the mountain, the Long Haired Girl kneeling before the Spirit King, he spoke: "You have told the secret of my mountain water. Now you will die!"

"I shall gladly die for the sake of my people."

"Place yourself under the waters."

"I will gladly place myself under the waters so that the water can bring life to my village. But first, can I please return home just once more to care for my mother?"

"Oh ... all right. But, if you do not return, I shall kill all the villagers! Now be gone. I never want to see you again!"

Once again, the Long Haired Girl found herself at the foot of the mountain.

"Oh, look how green my village has become!"

Indeed, gardens sprinkled with water grew strong and green to nurture families, and children were splashing and giggling as they played in the creek.

When the Long Haired Girl got home, she gave her mother a cup of the sweet water:

"Mother, now that the water has come to the village, I have time to visit my friends ... uh ... across the mountain. I've asked the neighbors to take care of you while I'm gone. We'll both be fine."

And the Long Haired Girl turned to wipe away her tears.

"I'm going now, Mother."

When the Long Haired Girl stopped to rest up on the mountain, she bid her farewell to her friends. But, suddenly, a little Green Man appeared!

"Long Haired Girl, I have been watching you. You are a very kind person. Do not worry. I have made a statue to look just like you. We will place the statue under the water and that Spirit King will not know the difference between you and the statue of stone. All I need is your long white hair."

The little Green Man pulled and tugged on the Long Haired Girl's hair. Once it was removed, he placed it on the head of the statue. It took root and began to grow.

Suddenly, the Long Haired Girl's head began to itch, and her own hair began to grow.

The Long Haired Girl watched the little man carry the statue to the top of the mountain, place it under the water, the Long Haired Girl's white hair flowing in the stream.

"Long Haired Girl, you can go home now, go home to you mother!"

The Long Haired Girl ran all the way down the mountain, her long black hair flowing in the wind, home to her green village, and home to her mother.

244

In the 1970s, **Nancy Wang** began as a dancer, choreographer, and teacher of modern dance under Gloria Unti, SF Performing Arts Workshop, who taught her to create work that is meaningful and addresses the burning issues of our time. In 1981, she began her partnership with Robert Kikuchi-Yngojo in So. Filipino traditional Kulintang music and dance. In 1987, they began storytelling as Eth-Noh-Tec, focusing on pan-Asian folktales and contemporary Asian American stories. Nancy is also a retired psychotherapist who is in love with her grandson!

Marguerite Renews Her Driver's License

ANDY OFFUTT IRWIN

THREE WEEKS BEFORE HER EIGHTY-FIFTH BIRTHDAY, Marguerite's morning alarm went off at 6:30, a half-hour earlier than usual. Within the dialogue of her mind came her mother's voice. "Get it over with." That's what her mother would say when Marguerite was a little girl met with an arduous task or an appointment. Upon hearing—*feeling*—her mother's voice, Marguerite said aloud, "O joy! O rapture!"

And then Marguerite heard her mother respond in kind, "O joy! O Rapture!"

Marguerite rose to get ready for her morning's errand, a task that felt like an appointment. *Appointment* is a word Marguerite avoids. *Appointment* is a word of childhood dread, a word she has always associated with going to the dentist. When Marguerite was a little girl, on those appointed days, her mother would sit on her bed and wake her up by saying, "Honey, you have a dentist appointment. I made it for early in the morning ... So you can *get it over with*."

Marguerite could hardly abide it when her mother completed the dreaded appointment announcement with, *get it over with*; there was too much of a lilt in her motherly voice, and she would smile a little too sweetly, feigning a sort of elation, as if *getting it over with* was to be met with something resembling bliss. At least Marguerite's mother had the mercy to keep a dentist appointment a secret until she woke her up on the day of.

To Marguerite's adult recollection, as soon as her permanent molars had come in, two cavities appeared. Had she been, what, seven? ... eight years old? Yes, for the fillings, she was given shots of Novocain by Dr. Nash. But the shots hurt, and she swears to this day that she could feel the pain of the drill. And even if she didn't have a cavity, the same monstrous belt-driven machine with its multi-jointed arm was used for the cleanings. In the place of the drill bit, there was a spinning rubber cleaning head that ground sandy paste into her teeth, as the base of her skull pressed into those old stabilizing cups that felt like a pair of fists.

When Marguerite was eleven, one of those *getting-it-over-with* mornings arrived. She was already a little bit awake when she felt her mother sit on her bed. Right after her mother finished announcing the appointment, and the customary *get it over with*, Marguerite sprang up, giving her mother a startle. Marguerite clasped her hands under her chin like Lillian Gish and gushed, "Oh, thank you, Mother. I'm getting it over with! O joy! O rapture!"

Six months later, when the next dental appointment arrived, Marguerite's mother woke her daughter by sing-songing, "O joy! O rapture!"

And so it was from then on, for any appointment or daunting task mentioned by either Marguerite or her mother, both would sing, *O joy! O rapture!*

Now, of course, in her advanced age, Marguerite knows the value of having a lighter heart on the other side of ... an *appointment*.

As Marguerite got up to make her coffee, she felt the old pang of grief in missing her mother. She wished she could tell her that she was aware of the *getting-it-over-with* lesson, a lesson that had been sweetened by her mother playing along all those years ago. As Marguerite sliced a banana into her oatmeal, she did some quick subtraction. 2007 minus 1894—her mother would be 113 years old. Marguerite chuckled at herself with that lump in her throat. She poured her coffee, lifted her mug, and said aloud, "Here's to you, Ma. I have to get my driver's license renewed today. O joy. O rapture."

Marguerite's driver's license would expire on her eighty-fifth birthday. So, for the final time—what she knew was one of many *final times*—she drove to that government office that occupies half a wing of her daughter's old middle school. Constructed in the 1950s, the school had once been sun-filled and breezy, but the windows had been covered up in the 1980s when it was retrofitted with air conditioning. With the construction of new schools following the county's population growth in the 1990s, the building was no longer desired as a school. Now unsustainable to tear down because of the asbestos, this dreary structure is well suited for this dreary errand. As Marguerite approached the building, she paused at the sign on the door and its overly-cheerful graphic design: a line drawing of an automobile made with the slanting initials for *Department of Driver Services*: *DDS*, which to her mind has always stood for *Doctor of Dental Surgery*. Marguerite had no choice but to utter, yet again, "O joy! O rapture!" as she opened the door.

Just inside was a machine on a post with a sign that bade her to push a button for service. Marguerite obeyed and pulled the numbered slip of paper that spat out before her.

She sat down among the other drivers and opened her purse to retrieve the license, which would serve as her identification for her *new* license. Back in 1939, when her Papa carried her to the courthouse to get her first driver's permit, her name in the family Bible, inscribed there by her grandmother on the day she was born, was her legal form of identification. All of her subsequent driver's licenses, voter registration cards, airline boarding passes, and proof to obtain a copy of her birth certificate so she could obtain a passport harken back to her grandmother's hand in that old holy book. She is who she is, born when she was born. So says her grandmother; so says God.

When Marguerite was sixteen, and it was time to get her first license, part of the exam would be driving around the square with a strange man in the passenger seat. Young Marguerite thought of the exam as a mere formality. She had begun driving her father's old "Dodge Brothers" truck around the farm as soon as she could reach the pedals. She could back a trailer by the time she was fourteen. Parallel parking was the same skill required for angling into the overly-tight space between trees that was occupied by the farm's hand-cranked gas pump.

The only new skill she would have to demonstrate for her driving test was the proper hand signals for turning and stopping:

LEFT TURN: the left arm is straight out the window.

RIGHT TURN: the left arm out the window, elbow bent with the hand pointing up.

STOP: the left arm out the window, elbow bent, hand pointing down.

Marguerite and her three closest friends, Mary Frances, Joy, and Tootsie, were all going to celebrate their sixteenth birthdays within two months of one another, so it was agreed that the three of them would apply for their driver's licenses on the same day. During the week before their tests, after school, these four friends marched on the sidewalk from the school to City Pharmacy two-a-breast (or, four-a-bosom as Tootsie, the saltiest of the quartet, was wont to say), each giving those required drivers' hand signals at every turn or stop. At the drugstore, the girls would show their mettle by consuming lemon sours: fresh lemon juice and soda water on ice. No sugar. Charles, the soda jerk, a classmate to all three girls, always rushed to arrive at the drugstore just before the quartet so he could serve them. Playing into the audaciousness of their conspicuous order when they entered, he always called out, "Four Lemon sours, coming right up!"

Charles's own lemon sour recipe required three lemons which he juggled, finally arcing each lemon onto the cutting board, where he sliced each one in half with a single stroke of the old knife that he kept finely honed.

Sixteen-year-old Charles, with a hopeless thespian's heart, harbored a secret three-fold life plan, a plan he had been plotting since the summer he turned fourteen years old. That June, his father, a college librarian, had been invited to attend a conference at Columbia University. The trip to New York expanded into a great father-and-son vacation. Charles's father insisted that his son's first Broadway play would be Hamlet, performed by the English actor John Gielgud at The Empire Theatre on 41st Street.

To Charles, the theatre was a palace. The actors were louder than he expected them to be, not yelling, but their voices were *larger*. He didn't understand the meaning of all the words, but he followed the story. The Denmark King's ghost, visually created with a growing shadow from an unseen body and light, terrified and fascinated him. Gielgud's Hamlet filled Charles with anger. Pity. A deep longing sadness. At the play's end, when the spell was lifted with applause as the houselights grew brighter, Charles stood and thundered his hands together as Gielgud took his bow. The small-town boy from Georgia was the only person in the audience standing. Until he was joined by his father.

On the four-block walk to their hotel, Charles couldn't stop talking about the play. "Hamlet was pretending to be crazy."

Charles' dad said, "Yes, he was. In the beginning, he was pretending to be mad."

"But then, he *really* went crazy!"

"Maybe ..."

"I mean, he was haunted by his father's ghost, right? I mean ... Well, Dad, if you were rubbed out and came back to tell me to avenge your murder, I might consider it."

"That's comforting to know."

Charles said, "I think I want to be a Shakespearean actor when I grow up."

"Okay. We will have to break that news to your mother. She was just coming to terms with you becoming a baseball player."

"Oh, I'll still play baseball. I'll be a Shakespearean actor in the off-season."

Whenever Mr. Spencer, the pharmacist and owner of the drug store, heard Charles call out at the girls' arrival, the old man would stop what he was doing, write down on his ever-present legal pad where he was in the process of filling whatever prescription was being filled, and walk to the edge of the high loft where he was the master of all he surveyed. From there, he had the best seat in the house for watching Charles' show. Mr. Spencer didn't charge extra for the third lemon needed for *the sours*, one more than was required for plain old lemonade. Indeed, he purchased a new, larger cutting board that would accommodate the twenty-four lemon halves for Charles and his antics when those girls came in. Mr. Spencer was a fellow whose heart was enlivened by the exuberance of youth, and he was proud and happy that his soda fountain was an after-school hangout, as it had been for years.

With a flourish, Charles would arc each lemon half onto the mushroom-shaped sieve of the commercial-grade squeezer, twirling the big crank arm three turns with his right index finger, forcing the crank on the lemon with a "HA!" Marguerite suspected that he was showing off just for her. Then, one day, all doubt was shed when Marguerite's lemon sour—only hers—was garnished with three pink-purple sourwood flowers.

Marguerite gazed upon the flowers and blushed. When she lifted her face to Charles, she asked, "Where did these come from?"

Charles said, "From the creek bank next to the school." After a moment, he drew a breath and said,

> *More flowers I noted, yet I none could see*
> *But sweet or color, it had stol'n from thee.*

Indeed, marrying Marguerite Ivy Cook was the third

element of Charles's three-fold plan.

He would recite Shakespeare to her for the rest of his life.

(And sometimes, to this day, he recites Shakespeare to her from the other side of the veil.)

Charles grew to be a high school English teacher who didn't forsake the classroom when he rose to become a wise and beloved principal. He also directed the high school's theatre. And he was the baseball team's hitting coach.

At the Department of Driver's Services, the widow Marguerite was thinking of Charles when she took her eye exam, something all drivers over sixty-five are required to do. As she brought her eyes to the scope, she heard Charles' voice, clear as the temple bell in her garden when the breeze moves through:

> *To me, fair friend, you never can be old,*
> *For as you were when first your eye*
> *I ey'd,*
> *Such seems your beauty still.*

Yes, from one of Shakespeare's sonnets. She thought as loudly as she could so Charles could hear her beyond the veil.

> *Well, dear friend, these old eyes*
> *You ey'd—*
>
> *No longer matters it how they look,*
> *Matters it now how they see.*
> *In a year or two hence, lest unfocused*
> *On book*

I must needs seek
A cataract surgeon for me.

Andy Offutt Irwin lives in Covington, Georgia, where his mother, grandmother, and great-grandmother grew up. He is a storyteller, theatre director, singer-songwriter, and Shakespearean actor. Andy has been a featured teller multiple times at the National Storytelling Festival and is a recipient of nine *Storytelling World Awards*, two *Just Plain Folks* Awards, and the National Storytelling Network's *Oracle Circle of Excellence Award*.

Rosie's Boys

A STORY OF CHICAGO BASEBALL
DAN KEDING

BASEBALL IS THE MOST DEMOCRATIC SPORT. I mean, just think about it: if you are playing basketball and losing by one point in the last few seconds, you give the ball to your best shooter. If it's football, you pass to your best receiver. If soccer, you pass to your best scorer. But in baseball, if it's the bottom of the ninth inning, with two outs, the bases loaded, and you're down by three, no matter what, it's up to the next batter in line. Even if this player is your worst hitter, on *this day*, he might be a hero. No race against the clock, just one team versus another until it's over. That's why my childhood friends and I loved to play baseball. Football was hard to play on cement. Basketball was hard to play without a net. We didn't even know about soccer where I lived.

None of us were really particularly good at playing ball. We all had our good points, but none of us was a great all-around player. I could hit, but fielding was an adventure. I once tried to throw a man out at home plate and wound up hitting our third baseman. Tony could pitch okay, but he closed his eyes every time he came to bat. He needed a novena to St. Jude, the patron saint of lost causes, to hit the ball. Davy could throw great, but he rarely ever caught a ball that he could throw back into play. Frankie was bad at everything, but he hustled and ran harder than anyone else on the field. He yelled and hollered at every play, whether it was a good one or not. With Frankie, it was like having a cheerleader on the team. And so it was that our little team of fifth-grade misfits never had a chance in the summer park league. This organization had no coaches, and parents never came to the games. The umps were only high school girls who worked for the park. All of this eliminated the idea that winning was at all important.

Our team actually started out in the hole because we had only eight players. We got in because Frankie signed up first and then got in the back of the line and signed in again as his twin. Of course, Frankie didn't have a twin, but no one seemed to notice. If they did, they must have realized who we were, and it was just a kindness to let us play. They simply looked the other way. The really sad fact was that Frankie's imaginary twin appeared to be the better player.

On a sunny day, a couple of weeks before the league games would start, we were practicing on the little kids' field, with the older seventh and eighth-grade boys on the good field nearby. We had decided that we didn't need three outfielders. Instead, we'd have right and left-fielders that leaned toward the center. For Chicago, we were already ahead of the times politically.

At our first practice, we noticed a tall, lean girl watching us from the broken-down stands. We knew her as a seventh-grader. As we watched, she slowly came off the bleachers and stood right next to third base. She was taller than any of us and had that easy stride of a natural athlete, unlike the rest of us, who often tripped, falling over our own feet.

"Mind if I play?" she asked.

"Don't you want to play with the older boys?" asked Davy. "We're just a bunch of fifth graders." We were still in awe of the seventh and eighth graders and still young enough to be unaware of the notion that girls couldn't play baseball.

"They won't let me play with them because I'm a girl." She stared at us as if daring us to comment. "How about you?"

Tony shrugged his shoulders and said, "Sure, you can play with us, but I'll tell you right now, we're not very good."

"That's okay," she replied. "I am."

She dropped her worn-out glove to the ground and walked to the plate with her bat. She ground the dirt with her shoes and slowly swung the bat a couple of times, hit the old home plate, and looked up and glared at Tony. She was calm, determined, and as cool as Mickey Mantle. She stared as if to say, "There's nothing you can throw me that I can't hit." Her stare was so icy that Tony actually dropped his arms to his side for a moment. When he finally raised his hands and went into his wind-up, he threw a perfect pitch right over the plate. Her swing was a thing of beauty. It was like watching Joe DiMaggio as she hit that ball right on the sweet spot. We watched as it sailed over the infield, the outfield, over the fence, and onto the street. No one moved. Like owls, our heads just screwed around on our shoulders as we watched the ball fly. When they finally came back to face front, we stared at her as if she had just walked out of a spaceship.

Then Frankie went crazy, jumping up and down and yelling about how it was the most incredible thing he'd ever seen and could she do it again. She did. She hit ten straight pitches over the fence. Frankie had a new position on the team. He stood on the other side of the fence and threw her home runs back to us. Now we could retire Frankie's twin. We finally had nine players.

This amazing girl was just as good at pitching as she was at hitting. None of us could hit anything she threw at us that first day. When she realized that she had been accepted, not as an equal but as an Olympian god that somehow decided to play baseball with a rag-tag group of boys on Chicago's South Side, she started throwing pitches we could hit to get some genuine batting practice. She could play every position and play it better than anyone we'd ever seen in the park. She threw one of us out after she had caught a ball in deep center field. Her throw rocketed into the catcher, who almost missed it because he couldn't believe anyone could throw that far. And each time she hit, threw, or caught a ball, a faint smile would cross her face just for a sweet moment. We learned that her name was Rosie.

We had always played because we loved to play, but now there was something else. We played to watch Rosie. We were in awe of her power, her speed, and her skill. She played for the sheer joy of playing, and we were her supporting cast. Just being around her made us all better, and we knew it. We actually forgot the name of our team because soon, everyone in the neighborhood just referred to us as Rosie's Boys. Most days, Tony, Davy, Frankie, I, or the entire team would stand outside her house and wait so we could walk her to practice. We carried her bat and glove. It wasn't romantic, just sheer admiration and gratitude. She was so good, and she was playing ball with us.

We started to draw a crowd at our practices. The little kids at the park and some old, retired folks would come and sit in the bleachers to watch us as we went through our drills. They were polite whenever one of us batted, but when Rosie approached the plate, there was a hush in the bleachers. When she rocketed a ball out onto the street, even the old men who had followed baseball all their lives wagged their heads in amazement.

When the summer park season started, we tore through the other fifth/sixth grade teams like a swarm of locusts. Team after team fell to Rosie's bat, glove, and arm. She could jump so high that many a home run ball died in the webbing of her glove. By the end of the first two weeks, she had the highest batting average in the history of the summer park games. If there was a problem that she was a seventh-grade girl playing in a boys' league with a team of fifth-graders, no one ever mentioned it. Even the opposing teams and the umps loved to watch her play. Frankie once described watching her play as being in church.

The short summer park season was drawing to a close, and we had yet to lose a game. The high school girls who organized the summer league wondered what they could do for a grand finale. Rosie's Boys were undefeated, as were one of the seventh-grade teams. The high school girls, all huge fans of Rosie, pushed for a final game between our team and the best team of older boys.

The day of the game, we watched as the other team went through their batting practice. They were huge, fast, and glared at us like we had no right to be there. There was one tall, lean boy on that team who was good, really good. Frankie looked over and just sighed, "Man, do you see him? Rosie, he's almost as good as you."

Rosie's eyes narrowed, and she replied, "He is good. He's my brother, and he's almost as good as I am." Then she winked and said, "Almost." Rosie's twin was playing for the other side.

The game seesawed back and forth through seven long innings. Rosie had hit three homers, and so had her brother. Incredibly, I had hit one, too; so had Davy. At the end of seven, the score was tied. The older boys were getting nervous. The eighth inning saw both sides score one run each. Then, in the top of the ninth, Rosie's brother hit his fourth home run with two men on base. They jumped ahead by three. Rosie countered with her fourth homer after I had singled, and now we trailed by one run. Our next two players struck out. Then Davy hit a single, and Tony, eyes closed as tight as he could get them, hit one, too. You gotta love St. Jude. We had two men on, we were down to our last out, and Frankie was up to bat.

None of us could remember the last game when Frankie hit the ball. We didn't count on Frankie as a player. He was our cheerleader, our heart. The problem was we needed a hitter. Frankie looked as though he was on the Titanic and had just been asked to rearrange the deck chairs. His face was ashen, and his hands were shaking.

He walked up to the plate and missed the first pitch by a mile. He missed the second pitch, too. The older boys were all smiles. The game was ending just the way they wanted it. Then Rosie called time out. She walked over to Frankie and gave him her bat. Then she leaned over him and whispered something into his ear. Frankie nodded his head and walked back to the batter's box. He swung her bat a couple of times, hit the plate, and then looked up with that same icy stare that Rosie always had when she batted. The pitcher looked like he was caught off guard, but then he went into his wind up and, as he let loose of the ball, Frankie yelled at the top of his lungs. The bat came forward and hit that ball with a crack, sending it deep into center field, where it bounced off the fence. Frankie stopped at second while Tony and Davy easily scored. The game was over. We had won. Frankie was screaming and jumping up and down on top of second base. Rosie's brother and his team shook our hands, and he even gave his sister a hug. Sure, he wanted to win, but you could tell he was proud of her.

We all wanted to know why Rosie had given Frankie her bat.

"I could see he was swinging too fast. I gave him my heavier bat. There was a chance it might slow him down," she said.

We turned to Frankie and asked what she whispered to him.

"Just look at the pitcher as if he was a bully, and you are standing up to him," he said.

As we left the field, we watched Rosie and her brother walking home arm in arm.

When school started, we'd see Rosie in the hall or on the playground; she always waved and smiled. She didn't come back to the park league the next year. She didn't have to. She proved what she had set out to prove, and none of us ever forgot it.

Rosie had given eight kids who loved a game a gift that was to last a lifetime, the gift of possibilities.

Dan Keding, lives in Urbana, Illinois, with his wife, Tandy Lacy. He tells revealing folktales from around the world. However, as an Illinois teller, Dan's strength is in delivering tales about his childhood in South Chicago. He is also an author and has been featured at storytelling events throughout the United States and in other countries. Dan is a recipient of the National Storytelling Network's Circle of Excellence Award.

All Dogs Go to Heaven

Kanute Rarey

WHENEVER I SEE LIGHTNING FLASHING in the distant mountains and hear thunder rolling across a dark, cloudy sky, I think of my "wonder" dog, Sport.

When my brothers, Ike and Fred, and I were small (about three, five, and seven), we had a family pet, an incredible dog named Sport. Oh, at least we thought he was incredible. In our small part of the world of childhood and in our eyes, Sport was a "wonder" dog. He was a working dog on our family farm, and he could run, jump, herd, and fetch with boundless energy.

Each of us could take turns throwing a stick and playing fetch with Sport until our arms wore out, and that dog would still be going strong. Sport could also jump a fence or gate from the barnyard to a feedlot or field in a

265

single bound. Grandpa and Dad could send Sport to the field to get our cows, pigs, or sheep. That darn dog would run circles around those animals until they got dizzy, and then he walked them to the barn in single file. Sport was half Lassie, half Rin Tin Tin, and half Scooby-Doo! We loved that dog!

But, like all dogs, cats, and other pets, after a long, long life, Sport passed away. That was many, many years ago, but I still remember.

Now, it is a plain, indisputable fact that all dogs go to heaven. I am less certain about cats since cats seem to spend most of their time living like they already are in heaven while still on Earth chasing mice, lying around on laps and pillows, taking naps and getting fed, while other folks take out their garbage.

But I am sure that Sport is up there in heaven right now. I can imagine that on his way to heaven, Sport crossed that rainbow bridge that all pets cross as they travel to heaven. They bound across the field of dreams and through the land of milk and honey as they climb that stairway to heaven.

As Sport ran through the pearly gates, there were dogs everywhere. Here was a dog park that went on for mile after mile and was bigger than Central Park in New York City. Now, Sport was a great working dog, good with family, friends, children, and farm animals, but he was a little shy around other dogs. It took him a while to not feel overwhelmed by all the dogs running free. Over the next week or so, Sport met, got to know, and made friends with lots of dogs, but four of them really stood out.

The first day in heaven, Sport met an old friend from home named Bear. The two dogs greeted each other with lots of sniffing and tail-wagging. His old buddy from back on the farm wasn't a working dog like Sport but a yard dog. There were always yard dogs around our farm. Sometimes they had run away from an abusive home, and sometimes they just got thrown out because no one wanted them anymore. Bear was one of those yard dogs who appeared one day out of nowhere and started hanging around. Once my grandmother fed him, he was there to stay. Yard dogs like Bear only did three things: eat and sleep and beg. Oh! Bear also chased cars. I said Bear chased cars, but I did not say he caught cars. Bear's name used to be Frisky, but after years of trying to chase cars and having tar and dust and grit and dirt tossed in his face by cars flying by on our old country road, we just called him Bear because he could barely run, barely bark, and barely chew.

Bear's fate was being a slow dog in a fast-car world. When Sport asked what Bear liked best about heaven, Bear said, "I love the all-day dog biscuit buffet where I can have all the dog biscuits I can eat, any time I want. And I love all the fluffy clouds that I find perfectly comfortable for napping. Oh! I can also catch a car or two whenever I want.

With that, Sport and Bear agreed to stay in touch, and Sport went on his way.

On his second day in heaven, Sport met Chewy, my Grandma's lap dog. Sport had heard of Chewy but being a house dog, Chewy never went outside, so Sport did not get to know her much since she was an inside dog that lived life in the house. Chewy was about as big as a bread box with sharp teeth, kinky hair, and beady little eyes. She spent her days on earth on my grandma's lap while grandma's spent the day in her Lazy Boy chair, watching daytime soap operas on television.

Chewy was part Chihuahua, part Dachshund, and part Komodo dragon. She would nip and bark and growl if anyone got too near Grandma. Grandma was under Chewy's protection. Although Grandma thought Chewy was her dog, in fact, Grandma was Chewy's human. That dog loved my grandmother, and the toaster-sized mutt spent a lifetime on grandma's lap, nibbling on Grandma's secreted dinner table scraps, chewing on a wide variety of parts of her body for God-knows-what, and protecting Grandma from unseen danger found only in Chewy's imagination! She was always watching out and rooting around, chewing.

When Sport asked Chewy what she liked most about being in heaven, Chewy said, "I sure am glad that Grandma and I could get back together again. Grandma came to heaven a few years after me. Now I don't have to miss Grandma anymore. I get to sit on her lap every day, all day long again. And I know she is safe, so I don't need to growl and nip and bite, and we will be together forever.

With that, Sport traveled on his way.

On the third day, along a path in the dog park just inside the pearly gates, Sport met a German shepherd named Sarge. Sarge was a stately, strong dog. He came to attention and gave a salute as Sport greeted him. That made

Sport curious, and he asked Sarge what he did before he got to heaven. Sarge said proudly, "I was an Army brat...a war dog. I come from a long line of dogs that helped protect the troops, sniff out bombs, and rescue folks. My ancestors fought in wars all the way back to World War I and before. I helped out in the Korean War and the Vietnam War—sniffing out bombs and bad guys. My pups helped out in Iraq and Afghanistan.

When I got home from my wars, I worked as a police dog. I sniffed out drugs, caught bad guys, and stopped them when they ran. And I protected my humans. As I got older, I became a therapy dog and visited nursing care centers and schools where I allowed folks to pet me on the head and pull my ears. And I laid my head in their laps. Now in heaven, this peace-filled world feels safe, and I'm not anxious, having to be on guard all the time. Now I spend my day playing hide and seek with other dogs."

After Sport had told Sarge his story, they parted ways, looking forward to visiting again.

On the fourth day, Sport came around a corner and almost ran headlong into a big, gnarly, grizzled dog. The big dog jumped back. Sport immediately introduced himself. "I am Sport. I just got to heaven. Who are you?" The rough-looking, growling dog said, "My name is Spike." Spike looked like he was part Rottweiler, part bulldog, and part grizzly bear. Spike apologized for all the growling and explained, "I spent my life at the end of a long chain in the back corner of the yard of my human family's house on a dusty, back-country road. I wore a big, bare spot outside that shack of a dog house I lived in. My dog pen was covered with old bare ham bones, chicken parts, and discarded plastic toys that I had chewed to oblivion. I wasn't treated very well growing up and I barked and growled like I would make mincemeat out of anyone who came too close. My chain kept me from getting away, and I was angry most of the time. I just wanted to protect my human family and probably would have licked somebody to death if I could ever have reached them."

"I'm free now. That is what I like about heaven. There is no leash law in heaven, and no chains are allowed. I spend my days welcoming folks at the pearly gates, playing soccer with my new soccer ball, and chasing butterflies and a cat or two when no one is watching." Sport just laughed, and they both agreed they had to watch out for each other and keep in touch as they spent their days in heaven.

On the morning of his sixth day in heaven, Sport was surprised when he walked by the pearly gates with his new dog friends on the way to the dog park and was greeted by a big, tall guy in a plaid shirt and work boots, leaning up against the pearly gatepost. He recognized the fellow immediately. It was that famous woodcutter and timber man, Paul Bunyan, and his sidekick, the famous blue ox, Babe. Paul and Babe were giants, legendary in all the logging camps across America for their help cutting, trimming, and loading timber on railroad cars and sending them to the big cities across the country to be used to build homes and buildings in all the new growing cities in the 1900s.

Sport and others did not know the little-known secret

that Paul Bunyan had always wanted a dog. And when Paul heard that our wonder dog, Sport, had arrived, he had been watching for him every morning and looking forward to meeting him. It was love at first sight.

Just as Sport and Paul saw each other, Saint Peter came to the pearly gates and threw out a basket full of extra lightning bolts. Without thinking, Sport and his new dog friends ran as hard as they could after the lightning bolts, grabbed them up, ran back, and dropped them at St. Peter's and Paul Bunyan's feet. Paul Bunyan said, "Good dog, Sport." That gave Paul an idea. He picked up another lightning bolt and threw it again. Sport and his new friends ran out to get it again. This time, even Babe joined the race to the lightning bolts. Paul and Sport became instant friends. Sport had always been a sucker for fetching a flying stick.

Now, when I find myself sitting in my rocking chair on my porch at the end of a long, hot summer day, and I look out across the mountains at the dark clouds building and the thunder and wind and lightning pushing through the sky, I wonder ... could that be my furry childhood hero, my old wonder dog, Sport, chasing after those lightning bolts as they flash across the sky?. I sure hope so. It always makes me smile.

So, the next time you see, feel, and hear the clouds and wind and lightning and thunder in the summer sky, maybe—just maybe—if you look and listen closely, you might see an old pet of yours up there too. After they crossed over that rainbow bridge on their way to heaven, running after that lightning bolt across the summer sky.

271

 **Kanute Ramey** stepped onto the storytelling stage after retiring from a long career in health care. He was born and raised on a small farm in Ohio. This bucolic, peaceful landscape served as the inspiration for his collection of family stories. Kanute points to the happiest, most joyful daily routines as a child, and to the sudden death of his mother when he was six, as stirring his rich reservoir of narratives. A dedicated friend to TSA, Kanute has helped with the annual TSA festival since 2017.

The Corn Queen

KIM LEHMAN

WHEN I MOVED TO AUSTIN, TEXAS, it was back in the days when I could move everything I owned in one car. You may remember those days.

It was my birthday. I had just moved to Austin and didn't know many people. I was sitting alone at home, feeling kind of sorry for myself. I was lonely, I was sad, and I was scared. As I sat there, the hours ticked away. Darkness crept into my mind and my heart. I became sadder and lonelier and oh, so heavy. Do you know what it is like to feel that kind of heaviness? Just getting up to walk across the room to pour a drink of water seemed more than bearable. As I was spiraling down, I thought I had to do something. Move. Do something.

Gathering every ounce of strength I could muster, I picked up my car keys and walked out the front door. The moment I stepped out of those four walls, with the blue sky above, the earth below, and my lungs filled with fresh air, I felt just a little bit lighter.

I got in the car and started driving, driving anywhere. It didn't matter. Then I found myself driving east of town. As if from nowhere, I saw a sign for Kimbro. Since my name is Kim, I thought, *that's where I will go for my birthday.*

I was traveling down narrow roads between fields. Then I saw a one-room church in the middle of a field. I pulled over, got out of the car, and started walking around the building, peeking in the windows. Who were the people that came here on Sundays?

As I walked around the back, I noticed a small ravine with a dry creekbed. I slid down the hillside on my butt and began walking that dirt-dry creek. I only took about two or three steps when I spied something on the ground. I bent over and picked it up. It was a fossilized shell bigger than my hand. It was a perfect birthday gift from Mother Earth. I took a few more steps. There was another shell, just like the first. Lifting the bottom of my shirt to make a place to carry them both, I took another step and another. Believe it or not, I found seven shells on the ground behind that church. By that time, my shirt was loaded down with these gifts. It was a little tricky getting up out of that ravine. Even though I was burdened with that extra weight, my heart was just a little lighter.

I got to my car and unloaded all my beautiful birthday surprises. Then, as I was standing there getting ready to slip into my car, I saw it. Across the ravine was a cornfield. It was beckoning to me.

Within minutes, I walked down that straight, narrow path between those corn rows. As I walked along, it was as if all the corn memories of my childhood came flooding back, and putting up corn with my family. We would plant and pick the corn. One person would blanch it. One person would cut the corn off the cob. One person would load the plastic bags to freeze.

Then I remembered playing in a cornfield with a little Amish boy named Daniel. He only spoke Pennsylvania Dutch, and my brothers and I only spoke English. But you know, it doesn't matter with kids. Play is a universal language. Those memories made me a little bit lighter.

Before I even knew what was happening, I shucked off all my clothes and lay on the ground between the cornrows, buck-naked in my birthday suit. Truthfully, this isn't surprising since my dad once took off all his clothes and streaked to the outhouse at a family reunion. I laid there so warm with the sun on my skin—all of my skin. The corn was blowing in the breeze like palm fronds keeping all the mosquitoes and flies off my bare body. It was luxurious.

Then I heard it. My peace was interrupted by the sound of a tractor. It was coming my way. Quickly, I slid back into my clothes and sat up. My head came right above the corn because it was May, and the corn was only two feet high. As I looked at that tractor, I wondered what the farmer was thinking, seeing a head pop up out of the field.

By this time, I was feeling so good. I arose out of that cornfield like a corn queen with silk hair, a tassel tiara, kernels of sweetness, and powered by renewed energy. As I walked back to my car, down that straight and narrow path, I held my head up high. And just like the Native American three sisters, I felt a little corny, full of beans, and never to be squashed.

Kim Lehman is currently on the Texas Commission on the Arts Touring Roster and is in demand as an effective workshop presenter with proven, cost-effective program ideas for librarians and teachers. She combines stories, puppets, music, and even science to facilitate her educational programs for children and adults. Her additional talents include playing the spoons and the nose whistle. Mark Wieland Photo.

The Spangler Cannon

SHAYNE LARANGO

I AM FROM TEXAS—BORN AND RAISED. My momma and daddy are from Texas. Their mommas and daddies are from Texas. I am no genealogist, but I do have the documentation that my great-great-great-granddaddy on my momma's daddy's daddy's momma's side was a co-founder and on the board of trustees of the first college in Texas, Rutersville College, chartered in 1840 when Texas was the Republic of Texas with embassies in Washington, D.C., Paris, and London. When I told one of my British co-workers that Texas had been its own country for about ten years, he turned, looked at me square in the eye, and said, "That explains a lot." Of course, he said it with a funny accent.

On March 2, 1836, Texicans declared their Independence from Mexico's Santa Anna—who was raising taxes, abolishing slavery, and naming himself dictator. That date is still considered a high holy day across the state, and yet, March 2nd, a few years ago, is the one the citizens of Spangler, Texas, will never forget.

That Saturday morning started off as beautiful and lazy as you please. I was still drinking coffee when I received a text asking me, "What is going on in Spangler?"

Before I could reply, the texts were coming in rapid-fire:

"There is a situation."

"Are you safe?"

"Spangler's all over the news."

I was headed to the living room to turn on the TV when I heard the helicopters outside, and a sinking feeling rose from the pit of my stomach. This can't be good.

Turns out, Virgil Renfro had moved into town, brought his cannon with him, and decided he wanted to commemorate Texas Independence Day by stuffing it full of gunpowder and shooting it off. To be clear, if you don't put some kind of projectile in the cannon, it is usually harmless. We Texans like to think of cannons as big, reusable firecrackers unless we need them for something else.

However, Virgil got a little zealous packing the gunpowder that morning. When he lit off that cannon, it made a BOOM, and I mean a BIG BOOM. The percussion shattered windows in all directions, and 911 calls started flooding in.

People thought a bomb had gone off or there had been a gas explosion. I mean, there was fear, real fear. And being just an hour southeast of Dallas, it didn't take long for the news media and the helicopters to show up and start reporting before anybody really knew what had happened.

In small-town Texas, we have our own sources of more accurate information than the news outlets tend to give us. Personally, I have a friend who listens to the police scanner all the time, I have a friend on the prayer chain at church, and my best friend owns the Lunchroom. The Lunchroom is located just off the square in an old historic schoolhouse, and it is where the citizens of Spangler hold court from 11:00 a.m. to 2:00 p.m. (every day but Sunday) over chicken fried steak with cream gravy.

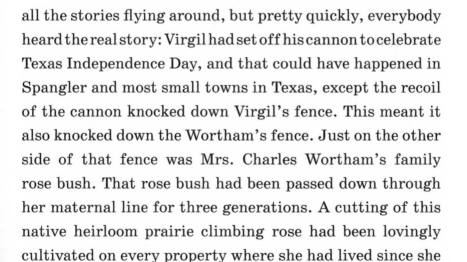

That Saturday was pretty stressful and chaotic with all the stories flying around, but pretty quickly, everybody heard the real story: Virgil had set off his cannon to celebrate Texas Independence Day, and that could have happened in Spangler and most small towns in Texas, except the recoil of the cannon knocked down Virgil's fence. This meant it also knocked down the Wortham's fence. Just on the other side of that fence was Mrs. Charles Wortham's family rose bush. That rose bush had been passed down through her maternal line for three generations. A cutting of this native heirloom prairie climbing rose had been lovingly cultivated on every property where she had lived since she left her momma's—including her sorority house. Her rose bush was also poised to win the annual Spangler Garden

Club competition for an unprecedented tenth year in a row.

Virgil Renfro could have easily gotten away with paying for windows and apologizing if it hadn't been for that bush.

Turns out that there isn't a law in Texas against possessing or firing a cannon without a projectile, and the police could only charge Virgil with disturbing the peace and causing property damage. Virgil paid for the damages right away.

The more outspoken people of Spangler quickly divided themselves between those who thought Virgil was just a good old boy honoring Texas and those who thought he should go to prison for scaring folks and plowing under Mrs. Wortham's rose bush.

The latter thought if they would just look hard enough, they would be able to find an old ordinance, a statute, or a declaration that would hold Virgil's feet to the fire instead of letting him off scot-free. They started having meetings at the Lunchroom to report their discoveries to Mrs. Daniel Forrester, who had a way of making herself the center of every controversy in town. Instead of a gavel, she clanged her spoon inside her tea glass, pretending she was mixing in her artificial sweetener. "Attention. Attention." She wanted to know if anybody had found a precedent to hold Virgil Renfro accountable.

The justice of the peace, who was sitting in on the meetings to keep informed of things, said, "Well, I didn't find a word about cannons, but did you know an old boy that fought in the Texas Revolution was buried in the city cemetery? They have a monument on his grave and everything."

Everybody in the Lunchroom sat up a little straighter with the news of a revolutionary soldier in their midst, but nobody else had found anything about cannons.

The next time they met, things also started off with Mrs. Forrester's spoon-clanging. "Things are getting off course. Who got the Scouts to make a grave directory of the entire cemetery looking for more famous people?" When nobody owned up to it, she finally moved on and asked if anyone had found anything pertaining to cannons.

"I found out that Spangler had a fort around the 1840s. I don't think they had a cannon, but Sam Houston camped there on his way to a gathering of Indian Nations," said the new seventh-grade Texas history teacher who had begun coming to the meetings to discover more colorful facts about Texas history.

There were nods of agreement and satisfaction because, geographically, that made a lot of sense. Besides, some Chamber boosters thought it might put Spangler on the map. In fact, after that meeting, Jimmy Joe Johnson took it upon himself and made a sign to hang outside his B&B. It said in big letters, "Sam Houston Slept Here." But in very fine print, almost unreadable, it said, "Not exactly here, but pretty close by."

The next meeting, Mrs. Forrester made her entrance in a huff. After her spoon-clanging, she said, "We are not doing all this research to make a profit." She was eyeballing Jimmy Joe's wife, Darlene, when she said it. "Please tell me that somebody has found out something we can use to bring a case against Virgil for his reckless endangerment." There was silence. Chairs were shuffled.

Then, from the back of the room, the traveling librarian could be heard speaking just above a whisper. "Did you know Bonnie of the Bonnie and Clyde was once locked up in the Spangler jailhouse? She wrote one of her infamous poems they published in the papers right here in Spangler." The crowd went wild.

Mrs. Forrester had had enough. She started up with her spoon-clanging And chastising again, "Why y'all act like Spangler could be a tourist destination!"

The President of the Historical Society was at the meeting, and that is just what she did. She put together a tour of Spangler, including the Spangler Cannon Incident, and started charging twenty-five dollars a head. Almost immediately, people started coming in from as far away as San Angelo. It was definitely good for business, but all those foreigners coming to Spangler caused a disruption to daily life.

In an effort to preserve tradition and get things back to the way they were, the Spangler Garden Club sympathizers bent the rules a little bit, and they awarded Mrs. Charles Wortham's native heirloom prairie climbing rose a prize for the ten-year record—in Memoriam. And things kept changing.

The next year, the reign of Mrs. Wortham's rose bush was upset by a hippie from Ft. Worth who moved to town, uprooted all the glorious St. Augustine in her yard and planted a xeriscape.

This year, Spangler got a story in *Texas Highways*, and next April, Spangler is putting on a reenactment of the Battle of San Jacinto. As an act of contrition, Virgil Renfro donated his cannon to the Texas Revolutionaries to use in the reenactment. However, Mrs. Forrester never gave up her fight in the court of public opinion, and from what I hear, that cannon is going to make headlines around the world.

Shayne Larango debuted at the 2016 Texas Storytelling Festival as the Dallas Storytelling Guild's Rising Star with her story "The Spangler Cannon." In 2018, she won the coveted title *Biggest Liar in Texas,* prior to entering politics. Shayne received the distinguished title Grand Mother in 2021 and again in 2022. She once woke up from anesthesia yelling, "I've got something to say!" and she still does.

Just a Summer Night

SAM PAYNE

THIS STORY IS A BIT OF A FANTASY featuring the actual people with whom I grew up and the place where it happened. The story imagines us as just a little older than we were when we went to church dances every third Saturday in American Fork. Jenny Jacobsen, with whom I rode the bus every day to junior high school, is assigned behaviors here that we only dreamed we were brave enough for. In real life, we were made more of longing than of action. But did we dance? Boy, did we. I can see us all now—dancing and dancing and dancing.

It's easy to find yourself in the doldrums in the middle of a long, cold, dry, grey winter. Everybody feels it. I feel it. My wife, Suzanne, feels it. The leadership of our church

284

congregation feels it too. Each year it seems, in the middle of January, they even assign a well-intentioned committee to wonder what can be done to help the members of the congregation keep their chins up until spring.

In fairness to the seasons, summer can come with its share of the doldrums, too. But summer doldrums are easy. In summer, there are "cookie walks" on a Sunday afternoon, in which a half-dozen families in the neighborhood are invited to bake big batches of their best and serve them up on plates in their front yards. Churchgoers find out in the bulletin which neighborhood houses will have cookies, and everyone strolls through the neighborhood between those houses, munching cookies and chatting on the sidewalk. Summer is full of cookie walks.

Winter is tougher. The church committee usually winds up planning another breakfast in the church gym ("served up by the clergy! Won't that be fun?"). Another breakfast.

Not this year. This year, someone proposed something that got approved in a church leadership meeting. Then, in Sunday school, it was announced to all the congregation's adults by a husband and wife from the committee. The committee husband began. Tugging at his collar, he said, "On February eleventh ... um ... just in time for ... er ... Valentine's Day ... we're going to have a churrr ... dnn ... hmmfrgrmble ..."

All of us leaned forward. What? What will we do on February eleventh, just in time for Valentine's Day?

The committee wife, in a gentle rescue, reached for the

microphone and swung it on its gooseneck to a position too close to her mouth. As such, when she said, "We're going to have a church dance. For the grownups!" the voice boomed through Sunday school like the voice of the Almighty.

Nervous silence from the congregation.

"Won't it be … fun?" She read the room, and what she read there sapped her enthusiasm.

More silence.

"A … dance?" someone in the back squeaked shyly.

A man sitting next to me muttered something that sounded like, "I think I have a conflict on that …"

"You'll go," said his wife.

For a moment, there were echoes of similar, muttered conversations throughout the room: "Dance? I haven't danced in… I'm embarrassed to even … do we have to … Well, I'm not … I mean, really, am I? Not going? Well, if you're not going, I'm certainly not…"

Sunday school continued, but no one heard. There was going to be a church dance. For the grownups. Inexorably, February eleventh was going to arrive. And on that day, we were to dance.

As for Suzanne and me, we saved our own interaction about the announcement until Sunday school was over. Then, after the closing prayer, we gathered our things and, on our way out to the parking lot, looked at each other squarely. In that look, there was a silent conversation: one of us said, "Are we going to that dance?" And the other one said, "Maybe we can arrange to be out of town."

I should say here that we love each other, my wife and I. But while the gestures of love between us are many and varied, dancing, especially in public, has, for whatever reason, ceased to be one of them. Repartee, on the other hand ... Well, let's just say this was going to be easy: "Really, we would love to come, and it's just killing us not to be able to make it, but sadly we've had out-of-town plans on the calendar for months." We didn't even have to rehearse it. Heck, we didn't even have to discuss it with each other.

I've long held that you never know what's going to bring on a memory, and you never know what memory it's going to bring on. In the church parking lot, after Sunday school, I reached out for the door handle of the Subaru. I pulled it toward me. And suddenly, I found I wasn't holding the handle of the Subaru at all. I was holding the handle of the used Plymouth Volare my dad bought when I was in high school to replace the Chrysler Newport we'd inherited from my grandfather. ("They used to name 'em after cities 'cause they're about the same size," quipped the mechanic when my dad drove the Newport into the garage for what proved to be the visit in which the car is pronounced dead).

It's my memory, and in the memory, I'm fifteen. I've just climbed out of the passenger door of the Volare in Jenny Jacobsen's driveway. It's a summer night. The sun has just disappeared below the western horizon, and the moon has launched itself into the sky above the mountain peaks that rim the eastern edge of our town.

"You'll be home ... when?" asks my dad from the driver's seat.

"Dance ends at 11:30," I say, racing off. Behind me, the Volare pulls out of Jenny's driveway and heads back to our own.

Dance. It's the third Saturday of the month, and that means there's a church dance, open to all comers fourteen and up, in the neighboring town of American Fork, seven miles away. There's a real DJ and everything. The prep for this month's dance has gone per usual: I've been in front of the bathroom mirror for the last forty minutes. I've tried the pants, cuffed and uncuffed. I've tried the brown belt and the black belt. I've tried the sweater, and I've tried shirtsleeves. I've tried the tie tight to the collar button, and I've tried it loose with the collar button undone. With a palmful of mousse, I've wrestled my hair into wavy submission. There's no big wall mirror in our bathroom— just a little medicine cabinet mirror—so to get a look at the whole ensemble, I have to climb up on the edge of the bathtub. I do that about fifteen times: up on the tub edge, then down to fuss some more, then up on the tub edge again. It's good exercise, and I'm panting a bit by the time I'm done, but everything finally checks out. As a final touch, I step through a cloud of Chaps cologne, and now, here I am at Jenny's house beneath the moon. Jenny is the driver tonight (it's her first time driving us all to the dance— usually, it's someone's mom), and she's a little nervy.

"The driver is responsible for the whole evening," she says, hyperbolically. We climb into her mom's big

Suburban. It's got to be the big Suburban because, while I'm the only passenger right off the bat, we'll scoop up Bex Williams, Darren Dibb, and Kelly and Blaine Weigel before we leave the neighborhood. Before we get to the dance, we'll add Joel Brian and Jason Terry, and maybe Becky Hutchings if she hasn't already found a ride. A Suburban-full. They are, every one of them, watching their clocks until we arrive. Once we've got 'em, it's full speed ahead to the American Fork church, where the whole gang of us will burst onto the gym floor, dance, and dance. It is our very favorite thing. We long for it all month, and when every third Saturday rolls around, we explode to the music like fireworks.

But tonight, when we pull into the church parking lot, the building is dark. There are a few cars there, idling, while a girl (I know her from my Spanish class, but I don't remember her name) jogs up to the church door and yanks on the handle. She turns to the waiting cars and shrugs. No dice. A few more cars pull in behind us. Jenny rolls down her window.

"It looks like it's locked," she shouts to the newcomers.

No dance? On a third Saturday? It begins to sink in.

"It happens," says someone. "Sometimes the dance just gets canceled."

"Why wouldn't they tell us?" asks someone else. It's a silly question. Who are *they*, and how would they tell us? We live way over in another town. People come from all over the Tri-Cities Area (the highfalutin' name given to

289

American Fork and its couple of neighboring burgs) to the third Saturday dance.

A third voice: "Maybe the DJ had another gig."

"Maybe," says someone, lonely and small.

"Anyway, it's no big deal," says a voice—mine. I say it, but I don't believe it. No one believes it. The Suburban goes quiet.

I'm sitting next to Jenny. She's leaning forward, her forehead on the steering wheel. Under her breath, she speaks. I'm sure no one else hears it.

"The driver is responsible for the whole evening," she says.

I open my mouth to tell her that it's not her fault the dance got canceled. I mean, that's silly, right? But as I begin to speak, Jenny lifts her head and speaks in a voice that reverberates through the Suburban.

"I've got an idea!"

"An idea?" someone asks from the back seat, startled.

"Just wait," says Jenny.

She sticks her head out the window of the Suburban and waves. "Hey, everybody! Follow us!" she says. She throws the big car into gear. She turns her head to the window again, cups her hand to her mouth, and shouts, "Wagons, ho!"

"Wagons, ho?" asks someone from the dark of the Suburban.

"Hang on!" Jenny hollers.

We lurch out of the parking lot, trailing all the other cars in our wake—a dozen or so in all. Jenny drives to the outskirts of town, along the lonely road the neighborhood kids take when they want to see how fast their cars can go. The Suburban climbs that road to the wide, dusty bench that separates the lights of town from the edge of the foothills. Jenny pulls off the road onto the dirt of the bench. Before us, the foothills sweep upward to the mountains, the mountains to the sky, and the sky to the moon. The Suburban rumbles to a stop, and Jenny is out of the driver-side door, directing cars onto the wide, flat expanse of the bench. Like a traffic cop or a magician, she waves and points and gestures until all the cars are off the road and on the bench in a vast circle, headlights pointing inward.

Jenny stands in the middle of that ring of light. Dust swirls in the high beams of a dozen cars. Jenny takes a deep breath and hollers:

"Let's Dance! Right HEEEEEEEEEEERE!"

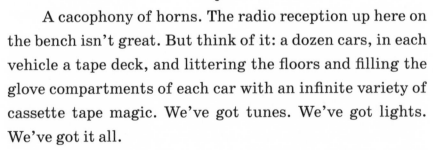

A cacophony of horns. The radio reception up here on the bench isn't great. But think of it: a dozen cars, in each vehicle a tape deck, and littering the floors and filling the glove compartments of each car with an infinite variety of cassette tape magic. We've got tunes. We've got lights. We've got it all.

And here, there's some fumbling around. These are, for the most part, cars borrowed from parents (the Suburban is, for sure), which means that many of the cassettes in these cars belong to our moms. It takes a minute of digging and a couple of false starts. Then, like a lightning bolt, someone holds up a copy of the Thompson

Twins' album *Here's to Future Days*. Hand to hand, it gets passed to Jenny. Jenny clicks it into the tape deck of the Suburban. At first, nothing but hiss. Then the electric guitars of "King for a Day" come careening through the speakers. The dust we're kicking up in the headlights is like a fog machine in a laser light show. The moon is enormous above us, and we are boogieing our absolute heads off.

There are forty or fifty of us on the bench, and just outside the ring of headlights our shadows are tossed high and wild on the hills. A dozen pairs of headlights make for a million more shadows than there are dancers. I know it's an illusion—that every one of those shadows belongs to one of the dancers in the ring—but to me, it's easy to imagine that they belong to a company of dancers much larger than our little forty or fifty. Innumerably more. In my mind, it's an army of dancers that includes our folks, their folks, and theirs—anyone who has ever been moved to movement by music—and isn't that everyone? In real life, a lot of those people are gone, and a lot of them have slowed down. In real life, they may not dance anymore. But tonight! Tonight, it seems like we're all here on the bench. All the people. The whole family. Not just a Suburban-full, but a world-full.

Maybe nobody feels that way tonight but me. But as for our forty or fifty, every one of us makes the same silent little vow as we jump, stamp, and sway: as long as anyone will let us, as long as there is music and moonlight, we'll dance in it. As long as we possibly can.

I dance with everyone that night, and everyone dances with me. I dance with Melody Johnson, her white Keds kicking up the dust, and I remember the night just a few third Saturdays ago, when we pulled each other out onto the dance floor, whirling and leaping and laughing and shimmying until the DJ pointed to us and gave us each a gift certificate to Rock's Records downtown, and pronounced us the winners of what we barely knew was a contest. (The next day, I'd trade my gift certificate for a cassette copy of Depeche Mode's new album, *Black Celebration*). That was a pretty good night.

I dance with Amy Bennion, her flowered dress spinning in the lights, and I remember the night just a few third Saturdays ago, when Amy and I slow-danced to "Crazy for You." When the music ended, we didn't let go of each other's hands for a long time. That was a pretty good night.

This one is better.

Eventually (about eleven-thirty, not to put too fine a point on it), one by one, the drivers of the cars gather their passengers, and the cars peel away from the circle, heading for home. Our gang climbs into Jenny's mom's Suburban and does the same. And while I'm not the last kid to be dropped off, I'm nearly the last. I get out of the car and turn back to tonight's driver. "That was a pretty good idea, Jenny," I say. And she says, "The driver is responsible for the whole evening." We grin at each other, and I close the door by its handle.

Only, suddenly, it wasn't the handle to the door of Jenny Jacobsen's mom's Suburban. It was the handle to the door of the Subaru, and I was regular-old grownup me.

It was after Sunday school, and I was looking at Suzanne across the top of the car. And she was looking at me as if waiting for an answer. I realized she'd just said something. Lost in old memories, I'd missed it.

"I'm sorry, Sweetheart—what did you say?"

"I said, 'Are we going to that dance?' "

I looked her long in the eyes. It seemed like just a minute ago, back in Sunday school, her eyes had said *maybe we can arrange to be out of town.* Or, maybe those were my eyes. I can't remember. In any case, whatever they had said before, Suzanne's eyes now said something else: *Might it be fun to go to a dance together? I mean, if you want to? I mean, it's no big deal.*

I looked at her. My mouth said, "Well, let's check the calendar." But I hope my eyes said something different. I hope my eyes said, *as long as anyone will let us, as long as there is music and moonlight, we'll dance in it. As long as we possibly can.*

After all, it's months until the next cookie walk, and everyone needs a way to keep their chin up until spring.

Photo by Aaron Cornia for
BYU broadcasting.

Sam Payne is the director of BYU Radio, host of *The Apple Seed: A Storytelling Podcast*, and a performing storyteller and musician. Sam can also effortlessly encourage listener participation. Once, when telling a story on stage about not being much of a dancer, he was interrupted by a seven-year-old ballerina in the audience who shouted, "Anyone can be a dancer, as long as you believe in yourself!"

To Educators

WALTER FISHER WAS AN EMERITUS PROFESSOR at the Annenberg School of Communication when he argued that all people are natural storytellers. To explain, his "Narrative Paradigm," published in 1960, pointed to the need for humans to make sense of the world. Making sense, he claimed, is accomplished by painting verbal pictures with words and gestures. To make these pictures meaningful to listeners, they must be presented in sequence and delivered in an engaging fashion. Sound like a story?

Notice the emphasis on "verbal." This is important because, despite the collection of written stories (personal and traditional) found in this anniversary volume, all the stories were delivered in oral form first. Many of the tellers represented in this book have their performances recorded on their websites and YouTube. It might be helpful to discover them to experience the oral telling of the story. We invite you to reflect, contemplate, and become absorbed by the stories created by these exemplary storytellers. Then, you will become a part of the story because their voices will invite you to enter the windows of their souls. Each will take you on a journey before returning you safely to the present.

The stories in this book forge connections among people and between people and ideas. Each teller shares stories about culture, history, and values that link people, and they do it through their unique styles. Each storyteller is authentic, harnessing key moments frozen in time and letting them thaw through their telling.

The collection of stories found in this anniversary book represents several genres and offers selections for learners of every age, every experience, and every interest. It is a priceless educational tool that will help students and novice tellers to develop a greater appreciation of language, cultivate skills and patterns in writing, spark an interest in reading, increase vocabulary, grasp a better understanding of culture, and develop a keen sense of imagination. And this is the shortlist. If you add in numerous examples of additional features necessary for compelling storytelling, such as coherence, resonance, descriptive word use, and how the love of story can reduce communication apprehension, then you have a precious find. So enjoy!

Thank you for all you do for our children and for your love of story.

—*Henry "Hank" Roubicek, B.A., M.A., EdD.*

Tributes

A Tribute to Elizabeth Ellis

In stories she is the wise woman, the mother, the seeker, the high priestess. Elizabeth was the first recipient of what would become the John Henry Faulk Award in 1986, honoring her significant contribution to the art of storytelling in the Southwest.

She served the Tejas Storytelling Association as its first President and as a member of the Board of Directors, reprising both roles when her service was needed over the years. She has also served as Festival Director, Artistic Director, and Managing Director, all multiple times, and she has shepherded many others in service to TSA. The organization has also awarded Elizabeth the Marvin Brown Volunteer Service Award, the Colson-Herndon Educator's Award, and the Martha Len Nelson Special Services Award. Elizabeth has served the Tejas Storytelling Association with unequaled dedication.

Her integrity, character and dedication to the Art of Storytelling and to the Tejas Storytelling Association know no bounds. Her tenacity as a creative problem solver and her dedication to grow our organization and nurture its storytellers has been a treasured gift. We have all benefited from that dedication, from her love of story, from her generosity of spirit as a mentor and a friend, and of course, from her beautiful and powerful stories.

Sponsored by The Tejas Storytelling Association

Photograph by Chester Weems

In Honor of the Late John Henry Faulk

Texan John Henry Faulk, with a hit show on CBS Radio, ran afoul of Senator Joseph McCarthy who was blacklisting performers. John Henry sued McCarthy's organization A.W.A.R.E. The Supreme Court found in John Henry's favor. He became a First Amendment advocate, using his humor to expose racism and pseudo-patriotism. The Tejas Storytelling Association presents an award in John Henry Faulk's memory annually.

Sponsored by The Tejas Storytelling Association

In Honor of the Late Finley Stewart

Having a dream is one thing; creating it is another. Finley Stewart did both. Founder of the Texas Storytelling Festival and the first Executive Director of the Tejas Storytelling Association, Finley created the logos and many of the traditions that are the Festival today. In 1990 he was the recipient of the John Henry Faulk Award. To honor his adventurous spirit the Tejas Storytelling Association Trailblazing Award was created.

Sponsored by The Tejas Storytelling Association

Photo by Wilgus Burton

A Tribute to Connie Neil and Barbara Fisher

 It is with great pleasure The Territory Tellers of Oklahoma place this tribute to Connie Neil and Barbara Fisher. While Connie Neil is the storyteller, almost everyone thinks of them as a team. Together they participated on both sides of the border. Connie served on the Board of Directors of both Territory Tellers and Tejas.

Together they for many years handled the silent auction at the Tejas Storytelling Association Festival in Denton. Connie was an early member of Territory Teller serving as president. Connie won the NSN Leadership Award in 2009 and in 2014 Connie and Barbara, as a team, were awarded the Marvin Brown Volunteer Award.

Connie passed away in January 2023 at the age of 93. His last live telling was at the 2020 TSA festival, where he told about the Red River Conflict.

Sponsored by The Territory Tellers of Oklahoma

Photo by Chester Weems

In loving memory of Martha Len Nelson

"Her children rise up and call her blessed." —Proverbs 31:26 Martha Len Nelson was instrumental in developing a deeper relationship with the City of Denton. She helped form the Denton Task Force which gave local support for the Tejas Storytelling Association. She also organized exquisite fundraising events which eased T.S.A.'s financial burdens. The Tejas Storytelling Association Special Service Award is given as a tribute to her dedication.

Sponsored by The Tejas Storytelling Association

Honoring Toni Simmons

Toni Simmons became the first African American Children's Librarian and Library Director of the Zula B. Wylie Library in Cedar Hill. Her storytelling gift was shared throughout the city not only to promote the library but to change lives. Her innovative programs propelled the library to new heights and community support. She and Traphene Hickman created the award-winning Youth Tellers program which has inspired and exposed youth to storytelling and storytellers locally and nationally.

Sponsored by the Zula B. Wylie Public Library

In Honor of Betty and Harry Berkey

Tejas Storytelling Association was very important to Betty and Harry Berkey! They contributed to the success of Tejas and they enjoyed every minute of their volunteer work! Betty served as President of the Board and as liaison to the Denton Storytellers. Harry served as Treasurer and produced many of the directories of our members. While Harry and Betty were wonderful storytellers themselves, they were exceptional story listeners. And, we all know, the world needs more of these!

Sponsored by Deborah and Scott Wilder

Honoring Dave "The Stringman" Titus

Dave "The Stringman" Titus is a Lawton, Oklahoma storyteller who for many years has done a youth workshop at the Texas Storytelling Festival in Denton. He delights and teaches children and adults about string art and how it ties to stories. One of the founders of the Territory Tellers in Oklahoma, David has travelled to over fifty countries presenting workshops and showing the commonality of string figures from different cultures.

Sponsored by Territory Tellers of Oklahoma

Photo by Chester Weems

In Honor of the late Doc Moore, "The Old Texan" 1939 - 2017

Joe "Doc" Moore, Ph.D. was, and remains, an extremely important motivator in Texas storytelling. A board member of National Storytelling Network and President of TSA, he spread his knowledge throughout the state and beyond. Long before storytelling guilds were common in Texas, he traveled from the Panhandle to Rio Grande Valley encouraging formation of local guilds. Doc was responsible for the birth of dozens of storytelling guilds. We forever honor the quiet leadership of Doc Moore.

Sponsored by The Tejas Storytelling Association

Photo by Chester Weems

In memory of our beloved Traphene Parramore Hickman

1933-2022

One of the founding members of the Dallas Storytelling Guild, Traphene served as our President. She had a gift for nurturing: listeners, youth tellers, and DSG members. Her dedicated commitment and hostessing skills were remarkable. Traphene will always have a place in our hearts and her heart in our stories.

Traphene Hickman began her library career telling and reading stories in the one-room library in Cedar Hill. She became the director of the library and continued to share her stories in her church, in schools, and at the library. She and Toni Simmons, master storytellers, are the co-founders of the award-winning Youth Tellers program. She was always an inspiration to all. Because of her dedication, the City's newly built library will be given her name.

With love from the members of the Dallas Storytelling Guild & The Zula B. Wylie Library

In honor of the late Tsagoi/T.K. Jennings

As a kid, Tsagoi/T.K. Jennings told stories. As an adult, he began a troupe of storytellers called Tipi Tellers and spread storytelling throughout Texas. He took the helm at Tarrant Area Guild of Storytellers in 2001 as president, told countless Stories Under the Stars, and was a resident storyteller with a MUSE library grant. In 2004, he told on the regional stage at the National Storytelling Festival.

Sponsored by Shelby Smith

In Honor of the Late Janet Latham

Janet Latham was a beloved supporter of the Tejas Storytelling Association. She lived abroad for many years. Her home was filled with interesting artifacts and some commented it resembled a museum. In 2000 she became librarian for WS Ryan Elementary in Denton. In 2001 she attended her first TSA festival. From that experience, she promoted youth storytelling. She was a Tipi Teller and started Li'l D guild 2015.

Sponsored by Li'l D Storytelling Guild, Denton, TX & Tipi Tellers, Inc, Denton, TX

Honoring Karen Morgan

Karen served as President, Executive Director, and Festival Director of the Tejas Storytelling Association. Armed with graciousness, commitment, and superb intellect, she led TSA into an era of growth by building bridges, creating liaisons and friendships with the Denton, TX community. Kindness and integrity defined her leadership. TSA is so very appreciative of all she did to shape both our organization and Festival. Karen's dedicated service and leadership went far above a call of duty.

Sponsored by The Tejas Storytelling Association

Photo by Chester Weems

In Memory of Dr. Ted Colson

Dr. Ted Colson was a founder of the Texas Storytelling Festival. He provided the practical voice of reason, so the event thrived. The 1992 recipient of the John Henry Faulk Award, he taught at the University of North Texas. Ted inspired students like Finley Stewart to become storytellers. The Tejas Storytelling Association's Colson-Herndon Educator's Award was created to honor him and those who use storytelling in education.

Sponsored by The Tejas Storytelling Association

A tribute to all the people who came together over the last forty years to nurture and grow the Texas Storytelling Festival

I am in gratitude for forty years of friendship, mentorship, community, and love in action—coming together and working together to build something bigger than ourselves. It fills my heart to overflowing. Thank you.

Mary Ann Blue

Photograph by Jacob Virgin

In Honor of the Late Marvin Brown

"The Youth Tellers are our future." —Marvin Brown

Marvin Brown gave untold hours of excellent service to the Tejas Storytelling Association for years. His unflagging passion was coaching and supporting youth storytellers who profited greatly from their relationships with him. Because of his dedication and commitment, the Service Award for volunteers was named in his honor. We evoke his memory each year when we award it to an outstanding volunteer.

Sponsored by The Tejas Storytelling Association

A Tribute to Mary Grace Ketner and Mary Locke Crofts

Mary Grace Ketner (R) and Mary Locke Crofts (L) planted a storytelling seed in the soil of collective passion and shared dreams. With determination, it unfurled its delicate tales. Nurtured by these gardeners, the San Antonio Storytelling Association began to grow, extending its roots deep into the foundation of story. For over thirty years, SASA has reached out, embracing diverse perspectives and talents, branching with a vibrant canopy of collaboration. SASA Salutes You!

Sponsored by the San Antonio Storytelling Association

A Tribute to Fran Stallings

Fran Stallings is an Oklahoma storyteller who has performed at national and international storytelling festivals, schools and libraries. She is known for her Japanese stories and environmental stories, and for her work in the EarthUp programs. A founder of Territory Tellers of Oklahoma, she was also on the NSN board, and headed the ORACLE committee. Fran, who has presented workshops or performed for TSA almost every year since the beginning of the Texas festival, was the 2009 TSA John Henry Faulk Award winner.

Sponsored by Territory Tellers of Oklahoma

Photograph by Mark Blumer

Honoring the late Lynn Moroney

Lynn Moroney was an Oklahoma storyteller proud of her Chickasaw heritage. She is known for her retelling of Native American sky lore, star legends, sky myths, and traditional folk tales. She worked with museums, NASA, and Astronauts.

Lynn was a founder of both Territory Tellers in Oklahoma and Wintertales, a major festival in Oklahoma City, for twenty-five years, drawing tellers from all over the US. Her work in Oklahoma City and Texas helped the development of the Texas festival. In 1988 She earned the TSA John Henry Faulk award.

Sponsored by Territory Tellers of Oklahoma
Photograph by Chester Weems

In Honor of Rosanna Taylor Herndon, PhD

Rosanna Taylor Herndon, PhD, received a Piper Professor Award for superior teaching.

In 1977, she began a second career as an award-winning storyteller. She was a charter member of TSA and founder of the Mesquite Storytellers of Abilene. She received the John Henry Faulk Award in 2018. Her stories are included in *Best Stories from the Texas Storytelling Festival.* Her collection, *The Line from Here to There: A Storyteller's Scottish West Texas,* was published in 2008.

Sponsored by The Mesquite Storytellers of Abilene

A Tribute to Eldrena Douma

Eldrena (Blue Corn) Douma was raised in New Mexico and Arizona among the Pueblo tribes of the Laguna, Tewa & Hopi, listening to Pueblo family stories. Living in the Texas Panhandle, Eldrena has been on the Boards of the Territory Tellers of Oklahoma, the Tejas Storytelling Association, and she is active in the Storytellers of New Mexico. In 2014 she was the recipient of the Tejas John Henry Faulk Award.

Sponsored by Chester & Velma Weems

Photograph by Chester Weems

The TSA Fortieth Anniversary Book Committee of Jaye McLaughlin, Hank Roubicek, Peggy Helmick-Richardson, and Chester Weems would like to make a special tribute to Parkhurst Brothers Publishers, for its part in development of *Forty Years of Texas Storytelling*. To them, this was more than a business project.

Ted Parkhurst has been a longtime supporter of the Tejas Storytelling Association. He has provided exhibits, moderated sessions, and given overall support for many years, and not just to Tejas, but storytelling across the nation. Ted and his wife, Linda, the lead graphic designer on this project, have gone an extra mile to see this book through to completion. We appreciate them.

Appendix A
FEATURED TELLERS

FEATURED TELLERS AT THE TEXAS STORYTELLING FESTIVAL 1986-2021 with some gaps in years. Those names denoted with an * are deceased.

1986: Ted Colson, Barbara Freeman & Connie Regan-Blake (the Folktellers), Zinita Fowler*, Rosanna Herndon, Elizabeth Ellis, the Storyweavers (James Howard & Finley Stewart*)

1987 A shirt with names on it is in the office: Jeanne Pasini-Beekman, Barbara McBride-Smith, Tom McDermott, Judy Nichols, Gayle Ross, Mary Carter Smith*

1988 Joe Hayes, John Henry Faulk*; Ayuba Kamau*, Doug Lipman, Lynn Moroney

1989 Milbre Burch, Gay Ducey, Michael Parent, Jay Stailey

1990 Len Cabrel, Rosanna Herndon, Beth Horner, Laura Simms

1991 Carol Birch, Allen Damron*, Heather Forest, Gayle Ross

1992 Charlotte Byrn, Ayubu Kamau*, Sarah McCoy, Jim May

1993 Jay O'Callahan, Susan Klein, Finley Stewart*

1994 Elizabeth Ellis, Rodger Harris, David Novak, Jackie Torrence*

1995 Jeannine Pasini Beekman, Charlotte Byrn, Ted Colson,

Allen Wayne Damron, Elizabeth Ellis, Zinita Parsons Fowler, Rodger Harris, Rosanna Herndon, James Howard, Baba Ayubu Kamau, Barbara McBride-Smith, Tom McDermott, Lynn Moroney, Judy Nichols, Gayle Ross, Jay Stailey, Finley Steward and the FolkTellers: Connie Regan Blake & Barbara Freeman.

1996 Jeannine Pasini Beckman, Michael Cotter, Bobby Norfolk, Jay Stailey, Jackie Torrance, Judy Dockery Young, J.J. Reneaux

1997 MaryAnn Brewer (Blue), Donald Davis, Patricia McKissack, Tom McDermott, J.J. Reneaux*

1998 Judith Black, Sparky Ruckers, James Ford, Kathryn Tucker Windham

1999 Shelly Kneupper, Lynn Moroney, Ed Stivender, Billy Teare, Liz Weir

2000 Linda Befeld, Dan Keding, Donald Davis, Dovie Thomason

2001 Rex Ellis, Heather Forest, David Novak, Tim Tingle

2002 Elizabeth Ellis, David Holt, Willy Claflin, Mary Gay Ducey, Judy Nichols

2003 Carol Burch, Gayle Ross, Kala Sojo, Kathryn Tucker Windham, Donna Ingham, Doc Moore

2004 Charlotte Blake Alston, Syd Lieberman, Mary Gay Ducey, Liz Carpenter*

2005 Blue Cooksey, Donald Davis, Dalton Gregory, Susan Klein, Baba Jamal Koram, Sue Kuentz

2006 Milbre Burch, Eth-Noh-Tec, Donna Ingham, Tom McDermott, Sheila Phillips, Antonio Rocha

2007 Peter Cook, Dan Keding, Olga Loya

2008 Carmen Deedy, James Ford, Doug Lipman, Donna Lively*, Doc Moore*, Tim Tingle

2009 Sheila Kay Adams, Sunny Dooley, Dennis Gaines*, Bernadette Nason, Michael Parent, Toni Simmons

2010 Linda Befield, Elida Bonet, Deecee Cornish, Eldrena Douma, Elizabeth Ellis, James Ford, Faye Hanson, Gene Helmick-Richardson, J.B. Keith, Barbara McBride-Smith, Tom McDermott, Dorothy McMahan, Lynn Moroney*, Judy Nichols, Jeannine Pasini Beekman, Sheila Phillips, Gayle Ross, Don Sanders, Toni Simmons, Jay Stailey, Tim Tingle, Shelly (Kneupper) Tucker, Nancy Burks Worcester

2012 Patrick Ball, MaryAnn Blue, Kevin Kling, Kim Lehman

2013 Willy Claflin, Deecee Cornish, Andy Offutt Irwin, Motoko

2014 Tim Couch, Janice Del Negro, Angela Lloyd, Peninnah Schram

2015 Elizabeth Ellis, James Ford, Barbara McBride-Smith, Gayle Ross

2016 Eldrena Douma, Rev. Robert Jones, Antonio Sacre, Minton Sparks

2017 Yvonne Healy, Dolores Hydock, Carolina Quiroga-Stultz, Don White

2018 Adam Booth, Beth Horner, Laura Packer, Tim Tingle

2019 Antonio Rocha, Twice Upon A Time, Josh Goforth, In The Spirit

2020 35 tellers for 35 years (Also the year that we cut off Saturday and Sunday due to Covid-19 and the mayor shut us down)

2021 Etho-Noh-Tec, Sam Payne, Heather Forest, Donna Washington

2022 Andy Hedges, Anne Rutherford, Deecee Cornish, Toni Simmons, Eldrena Douma, Tim Tingle, Donna Ingham, Carolina Quiroga-Stultz

2023 Joe Hayes, Elizabeth Ellis, Bernadette Nason, Sheila Arnold

Appendix B
AWARD RECIPIENTS

JOHN HENRY FAULK AWARD

The John Henry Faulk Award is presented annually by the Tejas Storytelling Association to a person who has made a significant contribution to the art of storytelling in the Southwest. It is presented at the Texas Storytelling Festival held in Denton, Texas every, and is the most prestigious award given in the name of storytelling in the entire state.

A native Texan, John Henry Faulk was a master storyteller, chronicling the stories and lives of friends and relatives through the years. Some called him an actor and imperson-ator, as he was able to mimic the voices and mannerisms of almost everyone he met. He was a satirist and used his humor to expose bigots, ignorant racists and ultra-patriots. But first and foremost John Henry Faulk was a defender of the First Amendment, and had the courage to speak his mind even when his was the only dissenting voice.

RECIPIENTS

2023 – Sue Kuentz

2022 – Tim Couch

2021 – Toni Simmons

2020 – Kim Lehman

2019 – Genie Hammel

2018 – Deecee Cornish

2017 – Traphene Hickman

2016 – Peggy Helmick-Richardson

2015 – Gene Helmick-Richardson

2014 – Eldrena Douma

2013 – Mary Grace Ketner

2012 – Mary Ann Blue

2011 – John and Rosemary Davis

2010 – Jay Stailey

2009 – Fran Stallings

2008 – Jerry Young

2007 – Donna Ingham

2006 – Dorothy and Mickey McMahon

2005 – Sheila Starks Phillips

2004 – Joe Doc Moore

2003 – Tim Tingle

2002 – The City of Denton

2001 – Tom McDermott

2000 – James Ford

1999 – Karen Morgan

1998 – J.B. Keith

1997 – Sally Bates Goodroe

1996 – August House's Ted and Liz Parkhurst

1995 – Barbara McBride Smith

1994 – Jimmy Neil Smith

1993 – Rosanna Herndon

1992 – Ted Colson

1991 – Jeannine Beekman

1990 – Finley Stewart

1989 – Gayle Ross

1988 – Lynn Moroney

1987 – Connie Pottle

1986 – Elizabeth Ellis

MARVIN BROWN VOLUNTEER SERVICE AWARD

Marvin Brown spent hours serving in the TSA office, volunteering his time with storytelling events across the state of Texas, as well as helping future Youth Tellers as coach and supporter. He is the epitome of volunteer service. Through his unselfish service he has helped TSA and contributed to its growth. The recipient of the Marvin Brown Volunteer Service Award is a person or group whose contributions of time and talents to TSA have enhanced the reputation of TSA in the greater Denton area and beyond.

RECIPIENTS:

2023 – Dean Keith

2022 – Larry Thompson

2021 – Fred E. Peters

315

2020 – Karla Sallade

2019 – Richard Nash

2018 – San Antonio Storytellers Association

2017 – Betsy Mosier

2016 – Valerie Kimble

2015 – Elizabeth Ellis

2014 – Connie Neil and Barbara Fisher

2013 – Jaye McLaughlin

2012 – Shelby Smith

2011 – Reba and Granville Ott

2010 – Traphene & J.R. Hickman

2009 – Dalton Gregory

2010 – Traphene & J.R. Hickman

2009 – Dalton Gregory

2008 – Janet Bickel-Burton

2007 – Debbie and Jerry Martin

2006 – Mel Davenport

2005 – Betty Berkey

2004 – Carrell Ann Simmons

2003 – Gene and Peggy Helmick-Richardson

2002 – Solina & Mike Marquis

2001 – Paul Porter

2000 – Peggy Capps

1999 – Marvin Brown

1998 – Martha Len Nelson

Colson-Herndon Educator's Award

This award is presented during a TSA Conference and is bestowed upon an educator who has given of his or her time and talent to mentor an individual or group in the development of storytelling skills or has been instrumental in promoting an appreciation or integration of storytelling in their field.

Recipients:

2023 – Maryann Blue

2018 – Elizabeth Ellis

2016 – Sue Kuentz

2014 – Janet Latham

2012 – Miriam Martinez

2011 – Trudy Hanson

2010 – Ted Colson and Rosanna Herndon

Martha Len Nelson Special Services Award

The Tejas Storytelling Association's Special Service Award is indeed special – recognizing that above-and-beyond kind of special service that some people are willing to offer to TSA and to the storytelling community in general. The award is not given every year because it is the rare person who demonstrates the level of dedication required to spend hours contributing leadership, organizational expertise, workshop instruction, story performance, and countless other volunteer tasks. Yet it is through the actions of these special individuals that TSA has become connected to and recognized within the greater story-telling community, while gaining recognition and leader-ship status throughout the state and nation. The services of this person have definitely made a notable impact upon the profession of storytelling as well as the visibility and contributions of the Tejas Storytelling Association.

RECIPIENTS:

2023 – Valerie Kimball

2022 – Brooks Myers

2020 – Peggy Capps

2018 – Mary Margaret Dougherty Campbell

2016 – Ted Parkhurst

2012 – Elizabeth Ellis

2000 – Harry Berkey

FINLEY STEWART TRAILBLAZING AWARD

On the 25th Anniversary of the Festival, the Board of Directors of TSA made a very conscious and deliberate choice to recognize the contributions of Finley Stewart, the man who founded both the festival and the organization. Each

Festival causes us to realize how many lives were influenced by his trailblazing spirit. Finley will never know what his actions created. The Finley Stewart Trailblazing Award will be given to an individual, group or business that created an outstanding organization, festival or business that promotes storytelling and utilizes the membership of the Tejas Storytelling Association.

RECIPIENTS:

2023 – The Zula B. Wylie Public Library

2019 – Hank Roubicek

2011 – Eileen Hatcher and Jim Ohmart

2010 – Rob Schneider

Appendix C

IMAGES OF TEXAS STORYTELLING FESTIVAL MOMENTS

From left, David Goodroe, Jeannine Pasini-Beekman, Elizabeth Ellis
Paul Porter Photography

From left, Karen Morgan, Paul Porter, and Peggy Helmick-Richardson

From left, Lynn Moroney and Jeanine Pasini-Beekman
Paul Porter Photography

From left, Finley Stewart, Deecee Cornish
Paul Porter Photography

From left, Rev. Robert Jones and ASL Interpreter Kate Lauder

Paul Porter Photography

From left, Gayle Ross, Jeanine Pasini-Beekman, and Kathryn Tucker Windham

Paul Porter Photography

Jackie Torrence
Paul Porter Photography

Dorothy McMahon
Paul Porter Photography

Gayle Ross
Paul Porter Photography

James H. Ford, Jr., Finley Stewart, Rosanna Herndon, and Ted Colson
Photo by Wilgus Burton

From left, Mary Ann Blue and Toni Simmons
Paul Porter Photography

Sheila Arnold
Photograph by Chester Weems

Saturday night concert
Paul Porter Photography

Concert stage set
Paul Porter Photography

Elizabeth Ellis performing on the Texas Storytelling Festival Stage (2023)
Photograph by Chester Weems

If you have enjoyed this book

point your browser to:

www.parkhurstbrothers.com